IMAGES OF ENGLAND

FROM THE CITY
TO THE MAYPOLE
A NOSTALGIC JOURNEY

FIRST AND LAST CARS
ON ALL ROUTES TO AND FROM CITY.

(Bank Holidays excepted.)

To City Weekdays First Cars a.m.	To City Weekdays Last Cars p.m.	To City Sundays First Cars a.m.	To City Sundays Last Cars p.m.	Route	From City Weekdays First Cars a.m.	From City Weekdays Last Cars p.m.	From City Sundays First Cars a.m.	From City Sundays Last Cars p.m.
5-0	11-3	9-0	11-3	Acocks Green and Albert St.	5-34	11-30	9-30	11-30
6-45	11-0	10-15	11-0	Alcester Lanes End and Hill St. (via Balsall Heath).	6-46	11-30	9-42	11-30
5-5	11-2	9-1	11-2	Alcester Lanes End and Albert St. (via Bradford St.).	5-39	11-30	9-36	11-30
—	—	10-22	11-0	Alcester Lanes End and Hill St. (via Leopold St.).	—	—	9-50	10-24
5-10	11-12	9-10	11-12	Alum Rock and Martineau St.	5-30	11-30	9 28	11-30
5-30	11-12	9-8	11-12	Balsall Heath and Hill St.	5-10	11-30	9-26	11-30
5-30	11-8	9-21	11-7	Bearwood and Edmund St.	5-37	11-30	9-51	11-30
5-0	11-15	9-59	11-14	Bordesley Green and Seymour St. (via Fazeley St.).	5-20	11-30	10-20	11-30
5-29	11-12	9-10	11-12	Bordesley Green and Albert St. (via Deritend).	5-50	11-30	9-30	11-30
4-45	11-9	9-5	11-0	British Oak, Stirchley and Navigation St.	5-17	11-30	9-27	11-30
7-30	11-17	9-21	11-17	Cannon Hill and Navigation St.	7-30	11-30	9-36	11-30
5-0	11-7	9-11	11-8	College Rd., Stratford Rd. and Hill St.	5-24	11-30	9-18	11-30
6-27	11-10b	9-6	11-10	College Rd., Stratford Rd. and Albert St.	6-10	11-30	9-0	11-30
4-40	11-4	9-0	11-4	Cotteridge and Navigation St.	5-17	11-30	9-27	11-30
5-0	d10-30	9-17	10-38	Dudley and Colmore Row (via West Bromwich).	5-54	10-40§	9-40	10-37§
5-38	10-34	9-34	10-34	Dudley and Edmund St. (via Smethwick).	6-16	10-16	9-36	10-16
5-15	11-2	9-0	11-2	Erdington and Steelhouse Lane.	5-10	11-30	9-10	11-30
5-17	11-17	9-4	11-16	Grove Lane, Smethwick and Edmund St.	5-37	11-30	9 21	11-30
6-45	11-2a	8-58	11-2	Hall Green and Albert St.	6-10	11-30	9-0	11-30
5-0	10-59	9-3	11-0	Hall Green and Hill St.	5-24	11-30	9-18	11-30
4-51	11-10	9-10	11-10	Handsworth and Colmore Row	5-14	11-30	9-30	11-30
5-30	11-10	2-0 a.m.	11-10	Heath St., Soho, and Edmund St.	5-50	11-30	1-40 a.m.	11-30
6-18	11-3	9-1	11-3	King's Heath and Hill St. (via Balsall Heath.)	5-48	11-30	9-26	11-30
5-0	†8-5	9-21	11-5	King's Heath and Hill St. (via Leopold St.)	5-28	h8-31	9-32	11-30
5-8	11-5	9-4	11-3	King's Heath and Albert St. (via Bradford St.)	5-39	11-30	9-36	11-30
5-12	11-16	9-12	11-16	Ladywood and Navigation St.	5-29	11-30	9-28	11-30
5-0	11-16	9-12	11-16	Lodge Rd., Winson Green, and Edmund St.	5-17	11-30	9-30	11-30
5-32c	10-52	8-48	10-53	Longbridge and Navigation St.	5-17	11-30	9-30	11-30
6-3	11-16	9-30	11-17	Lozells and Colmore Row (via Wheeler St.)	6-20	11-30	9-46	11-30
From Villa Road.					From Slade Road.			
5-41	11-30	9-30	11-30	Lozells and Gravelly Hill.	6-4	11-30	9-35	11-30
To City					From City			
5-48	11-9	9-5	11-9	Moseley, Moseley Village and Hill St. (via Balsall Heath).	5-48	11-30	9-26	11-30
5-15	11-12	9-11	11-12	Moseley, Moseley Village and Albert St.	5-39	11-30	9-36	11-30
5-6	8-11t	9-27	11-10	Moseley, Moseley Village and Hill St. (via Leopold St.).	5-28	8-31h	9-32	11-30
4-52	11-10	9-11	11-11	New Inns, Handsworth, and Colmore Row.	5-14	11-30	9-30	11-30
5-25s	10-58	8-55	11-0	Northfield and Navigation St.	5-17	11-30	9-30	11-30
5-36	10-51	9-31	10-51	Oldbury and Edmund St.	6-16	10-46	9-36	10-46
5-33	11-12	9-5	11-12	Oxhill Rd., Handsworth, and Colmore Row.	5-53	11-30	9-25	11-30
5-15	11-12	9-12	11-13	Perry Barr and Martineau St.	5-35	11-30	9-30	11-30
6-22	11-3	9-0	11-3	Pype Hayes and Steelhouse Lane.	5-20	11-30	9-30	11-30
5-32	10-42k	9-15	10-50	Rednal and Navigation St.	5-17	11-30	9-30	11-30
5-42f	10-50	8-45	10-46	Rubery and Navigation St.	5-47	11-25†	9-37	11-30
4-57	11-10	9-5	11-10	Selly Oak and Navigation St.	5-17	11-30	9-27	11-30
5-20	11-6	9-5	11-6	Short Heath and Steelhouse Lane.	5-28	11-30	9-20	11-30
6-5	11-13x	9-10	11-13	St. John's Rd., Sparkhill, and Albert St.	6-10	11-30	9-0	11-30
5-4	11-11	9-14	11-11	St. John's Rd., Sparkhill, and Hill Street	5-24	11-30	9-18	11-30
4-56	11-14	9-15	11-16	Stafford Rd., Handsworth, and Colmore Row.	5-14	11-30	9-30	11-30
5-44	10-58	8-57	10-58	Spon Lane, Smethwick.	6-16	11-26	9-36	11-26
4-54	11-8	10-43	11-8	Stechford and Seymour St. (via Fazeley St.)	6-51	11-30	10-20	11-30
5-23	11-6	9-4	11-6	Stechford and Albert St. (via Deritend).	5-50	11-30	9-30	11-30
5-5	11-7	9-6	11-7	Stockland Green and Steelhouse Lane.	5-28	11-30	9-30	11-30
7-0	11-12	10-15	11-10	Stoney Lane, Sparkbrook and Hill St.	7-20	11-30	10-35	11-30
5-9	11-17	9-9	11-12	Trafalgar Rd. and Navigation St. (via Leopold St.).	5-28	11-30	9-32	11-30
5-18	11-15	9-14	11-15	Trafalgar Rd., Moseley, and Albert St. (via Bradford St.)	5-39	11-30	9-36	11-30
5-26	11-7	9-4	11-7	Tyburn Rd., Holly Lane, and Steelhouse Lane.	5-20	11-30	9-30	11-30
4-57	11-11	9-10	11-11	Ward End and Martineau St.	5-24	11-30	9-31	11-30
4-55	11-9	9-8	11-9	Washwood Heath and Martineau St.	5-24	11-30	9-31	11-30
5-20	10-45	9-22	10-44	Wednesbury and Colmore Row.	5-14	11-10	9-30	11-12
5-20	11-15	9-2	11-15	Windmill Lane, Smethwick, and Edmund St.	5-37	11-30	9-21	11-30
5-17	11-14	9-12	11-13	Witton and Martineau St. (via Aston Cross). From Trinity Rd., Sundays.	5-35	11-30	9-31	11-30
5-35	11-14	No Service		Witton and Martineau St. (via Six Ways).	5-53	11-30	No Service	

x 11-11 p.m. Sats. † 11-30 p.m. Sats. b 11-7 p.m. Sats. § Gt. Bridge only, 11-0 p.m. weekdays, 11-9 p.m. Sundays. a 10-59 p.m. Sats. h 2-28 p.m. Sats. i 2 p.m. Sats. c 5-0 a.m. Sats. t 2-6 p.m. Sats. d 10-39 p.m. Sats. s 5-7 a.m. Sats. f 5-12 a.m. Sats. k 10-50 p.m. Sats.

IMAGES OF ENGLAND

FROM THE CITY
TO THE MAYPOLE

A NOSTALGIC JOURNEY

DAVID HARVEY

TEMPUS

Frontispiece: Timetable from Birmingham Corporation Tramway and Omnibus Department, 1935.

First published 2007

Tempus Publishing Limited
The Mill, Brimscombe Port,
Stroud, Gloucestershire, GL5 2QG
www.tempus-publishing.com

British Library Cataloguing in Publication Data.
A catalogue record for this book is available from the British Library.

ISBN 978 07524 4341 6

Typesetting and origination by Tempus Publishing Limited.
Printed in Great Britain.

Contents

Acknowledgements

The author is grateful to the many photographers – both those acknowledged in the text and others unknown – who have contributed to this volume. Special thanks are due to Peter Drake of Birmingham Central Library for his invaluable assistance, John Gillham for the use of the map and to Barry Ware for his usual informative nuggets of information, and finally but not least to my wife, Di, who has proof read the document and encouraged me to go on with the task.

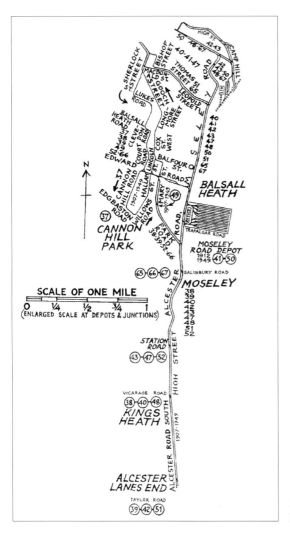

Map of the area covered by the routes in this book. (John Gillham)

Introduction

Take a journey through time from Birmingham's city centre to the edge of rural Worcestershire on the variety of public transport which has served Balsall Heath, Moseley, King's Heath, the Maypole and Druids Heath. The modern day A435 takes in Moseley Road, Alcester Road and Alcester Road South, but for many years, the back streets of Balsall Heath were also served by an intensive public transport system.

Background History

Initially the area was served by steam trams operated by Birmingham Central Tramways which later became the City of Birmingham Tramways Company in 1896. When the twenty-one-year operating lease held by the CBT expired on 31 December 1906, Birmingham Corporation Tramways began operation from the new Moseley Road depot on Tuesday 1 January 1907. The municipal operation of trams continued until 1 October 1949 when Corporation buses took over. Birmingham city transport department continued operations until they were compulsorily integrated into West Midland Passenger Transport on 1 October 1969. WMPTE continued to operate buses on the Maypole routes until government deregulation occurred on 26 October 1986 and the operating name changed to West Midlands Travel. As a direct result of deregulation, Smiths of Shenington began operating to Druids Heath on 30 November 1987 with their cut-price 50Y service under the operating name of Your Bus with a variety of second-hand orange, brown and white liveried buses. Briefly the competition between West Midlands and Your Bus led to bus frequencies of about two minutes in each direction along the length of Moseley and Alcester Roads. Obviously this situation became unsustainable with virtually empty buses being operated and during 1993 the Your Bus operation was sold to West Midlands. Meanwhile the West Midlands operation was subject to a management buy-out in 1993 and the company was sold to the National Express Group in 1995, changing its name to West Midlands Travel. Finally, the by-now orange and white painted Your Bus vehicles were absorbed into the main fleet on 4 February 2001.

Steam Trams

Birmingham's original steam tram service to Moseley was opened by the Birmingham Central Tramways Company on 28 December 1884 from Moat Row via Bradford Street and Moseley Road and was extended to terminate alongside New Street Station in Hill Street by way of Bromsgrove Street and the newly opened John Bright Street on 20 June 1885. The second steam tram route implemented on 19 July 1886 also started from Hill Street but went through Balsall Heath by way of Gooch Street, Mary Street and Park Road. An extension of about one mile was opened to High Street, King's Heath on 1 February 1887 which also served the Silver Street steam tram depot.

Electric Trams

There were two basic routes, the earliest ones starting in the Hill Street/Navigation Street corner which corresponded with the former CBT steam tram services and the later routes starting from the High Street/Dale End/Albert Street area which was much nearer the heart of the city. The closure of the CBT steam tram services led to the opening on 1 January 1907 of three new services running from the Navigation Street/Hill Street termini. They were the Alcester Lanes End via Balsall Heath which became the 39 route in the renumbering scheme of 1915. This was known as 'the Chinese Railway' apparently because of its snake-like progress in each direction through some of the worst slum properties in Balsall Heath. The branch off this route was the second service, the short circular 37 service to Cannon Hill by way of Willows Road. Initially the first forty of the radial-truck 71 class were allocated to the new Moseley Road depot. The third and defining route in the area was the 41 which went through Highgate and climbed the 1 in 13 hill in Leopold Street to reach Moseley Road which required that the fifty members of the 401 class were equipped with the Spencer-Dawson oil and air brake in order to prevent vehicles rolling uncontrollably down this steep hill. These four-wheelers replaced the 71 class cars at the end of 1913. Meanwhile on 6 September 1909, a new service began running from High Street via the Bull Ring, Digbeth and Bradford Street and into Moseley Road which was subsequently numbered 42. The city terminus was moved to Dale End on 9 November 1921 and finally to outside the Beehive department store on 13 July 1930. Various eight-wheeled, totally enclosed trams were allocated to Moseley Road depot from 1926, but the 401 class of trams were to become the last narrow-gauge, open-balcony four-wheeled trams to operate in the country. The abandonment of the tram services occurred on 1 October 1949 when car 386 became the official last tram on the 42 service.

Buses

The replacement buses were all brand new, exposed-radiator Daimler CVD6s with Metro-Cammell bodies, numbered 1931-1971 which were augmented by a number of pre-war Daimler COG5 double-deckers. The new bus services were: 48 to the Maypole from Paradise Street via Balsall Heath, Moseley and King's Heath, the 49 via Leopold Street to King's Heath (though the 49A short working to Moseley Village was the regular all-day service) and finally the main-road route from either Albert Street, Carrs Lane or High Street which was numbered 50.

Between September 1950 and January 1951, 'New-Look' concealed-radiator Daimler CVD6 2031-2072 came to Moseley Road depot and basically these quietly refined buses ran all the services until 1964. They, in turn, were replaced by some of the Corporation's first rear-engined Daimler Fleetlines 3351-3384 which ran well into the days of West Midlands PTE. On 10 July 1966, the 48 service was extended to the Druids Heath Estate. Moseley Road garage was closed by WMPTE on 5 March 1972 and the services were transferred mainly to Liverpool Street garage including the 50 which was still going only as far as the Maypole. A variety of Daimler Fleetlines, specifically those in the NOB---M series, were allocated to the routes, but throughout the 1980s the services to the Maypole were operated by Mark I and Mark II MCW Metrobuses. The competition from Your Bus led to the entry into service of forty Alexander-bodied Scania N113DRBs between August and November 1990, specifically for the number 50 Druids Heath route. Numbered in a discontinuous batch between 3201 and 3247, (H 201 LOM etc.), they in turn were replaced by route dedicated Volvo B7TL models and Dennis Trident II vehicles all with very similar Alexander bodies dating from 2001 or 2002.

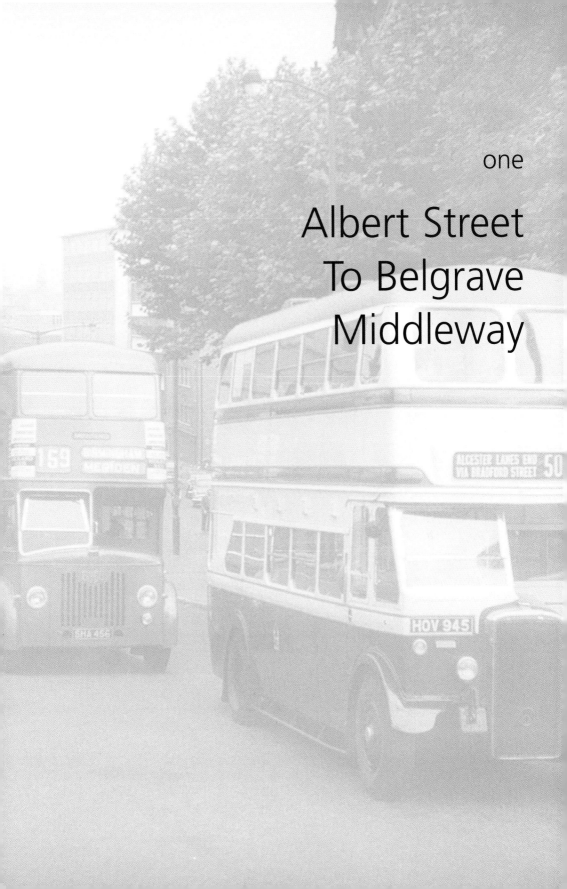

one

Albert Street
To Belgrave
Middleway

Just about to turn out of Albert Street and into High Street is 2051 (JOJ 51), a 'New-Look' front Daimler CVD6 with a fifty-four seat Metro-Cammell body. It is working on the 50B route to Alcester Lanes End in about 1953, not long after the bus services were redirected to travel up Albert Street. The bus had entered service on 1 December 1950 and is in virtually original condition with wheel discs and trafficators. On the corner of Dale End and Albert Street is Wake's fishmonger shop, while above it is the Royal Air Force recruiting office. (P.J. Marshall)

The main service from Alcester Lanes End to the city centre was the 42 route which terminated outside the Beehive department store in Albert Street. Known as 'a warehouse for the people', it was originally owned by Charles Richards, trading for over a century selling household goods, drapery and clothes until finally it finally closed on leap day, 1972. Standing next to the impressive cast-iron, glass-roofed shelters, tramcar 405, one of the fifty 401 class, United Electric-bodied trams mounted on Mountain and Gibson 7ft 6in. long trucks, loads up with passengers on 25 September 1949. (G.F. Douglas)

Nearly all of the fifty-four seats on car 441 are occupied as it leaves the Albert Street terminus, turning right in front of Moor House and into Moor Street where it will meet the inbound trams which will turn left into Carrs Lane at the Corner public house. 441 is working on the 42 service to Alcester Lanes End during September 1949. The tram has just left the terminus and swings into Moor Street. These trams were fitted with the Spencer-Dawson air and oil brake in the latter half of 1913 which locked the brakes on, preventing the tram from running away on a steep gradient. The 401 class cars were thus fitted to facilitate their safe use, particularly on the 1 in 13 gradient of Leopold Street. (A.N. Porter)

The 1955 Marks & Spencer building in Carrs Lane replaced an earlier store built in the 1920s and destroyed on 9 April 1941 in an air raid. After the abandonment of the trams on 1 October 1949, the replacement Moseley Road 50 bus route operated in a clockwise direction from Moor Street into Carrs Lane, High Street. It terminated in Albert Street before returning to Moor Street. This route was retained until 16 March 1952 when a number of services including the Moseley Road bus routes were re-routed to run up Albert Street and go via High Street into the Bull Ring. Bus 1961 (HOV 961), a Daimler CVD6 with an MCCW body entered service on the first day of the new Moseley Road buses. It can be seen here standing at the third 50 bus terminus, now at the Carrs Lane terminus, introduced on 15 March 1964. The 1961 is working on the 50B service to Alcester Lanes End. This bus would only use this new terminal loop for a few months as it was withdrawn at the end of July 1964. (D.R. Harvey collection)

West Midlands Travel ordered only one batch of Scania N113DR buses to be delivered to Birmingham Central garage in Liverpool Street. They were purchased in order to compete with the post-deregulation operator, Your Bus which had introduced a fleet of second-hand double and single-deckers with cut-price fares on the Moseley Road services. There were forty of these Alexander-bodied seventy-six-seaters and 3227 (H227 LOM), stands in High Street in October 1991 when working on the 50 route to Druids Heath. Alongside the bus is the 1950s Big Top site buildings and behind it the iconic 265ft high, twenty-five-storey Rotunda Building which opened in 1965. (D.R. Harvey)

3372 (372 KOV), stands in St Martin's Circus outside the entrance to New Street Station with the Bull Ring Centre and Smallbrook Ringway, as it was named in 1965, in the background. This bus is a Daimler Fleetline CRG6LX with a Metro-Cammell H43/33F body. Entering service on 1 July 1964, it was one of a class of thirty-four which replaced almost at a stroke all of Moseley Road garage's allocation of exposed-radiator Daimler CVD6s of 1949. The Fleetline is working on the 50 route and, despite the destination information, has just arrived from the city boundary at the Maypole. (R.H.G. Simpson)

Travelling out of the city centre along Moor Street is UEC-bodied four-wheeled car 414 which is working on the main line 42 service from Albert Street to 'the Knob' at Alcester Lanes End, King's Heath. It is about to approach the left turn into the Bull Ring having just left the tram stop outside Nelson House. On the right is Allen Griffiths' shoe shop which occupied the corner ground floor premises which continued around into the Bull Ring. (C. Carter)

The Bull Ring's steep hill and cobbled road sets made it very slippery in wet or icy conditions. Parked on the left alongside St Martin's Parish Church are two Midland Red single-deckers, the rear one being the 97 (OA 7097), a Tilling-Stevens TS3. Travelling up the Bull Ring on the 42 route in about 1925 is car 449 which is about to turn right in front of the early nineteenth-century buildings on the corner of Moor Street. At the top of the Bull Ring beyond the heavily laden horse and carts, the street stalls and the statue of Horatio Nelson, is the old Market Hall with its impressive, Doric-order main entrance. It was designed by Charles Edge and officially opened on 12 February 1835. It was huge, being 365ft long by 106ft wide with a capacity of up to 600 stalls selling fresh fruit and vegetables, meat, poultry and fish. The Market Hall was partially destroyed by incendiaries in an air raid during the night of 25-26 August 1940. Only the outer walls were left standing though it continued as Birmingham's main retail market until it was demolished in 1962. (D.R. Harvey collection)

The parish church of St Martin's stands near to the top of the Bull Ring. A church has stood on or near this site since before Domesday Book was written in 1086, when the lord of the manor's land was worth twenty shillings and supported a population of barely sixty people. The church grew up the market, the Royal Charter being granted in about 1166 by King Henry II. The late thirteenth-century sandstone church built by the de Bermingham family gradually fell into disrepair and the present-day tower and spire were built in 1853. A new nave and aisles costing £32,000, based on the medieval foundations were designed by Julius Alfred Chatwin in an attractive, well-proportioned, fourteenth-century Gothic style enlarging the medieval ground plan at the eastern end. This combination of the new 1875 church and the 1855 tower, plus a few remnants of the medieval building, is what has survived to the present day. Passing the tree-lined churchyard is one of the quiet Daimler-engined Daimlers CVD6s, 1945 (HOV 945), being employed on the 50B route, while behind it, storming up the steep Bull Ring hill is Midland Red's 4056 (SHA 456), one of the powerful Leyland Titans PD2/12. (R.F. Mack)

4226 (YOX 226K), a West Midland PTE Daimler Fleetline CRG6LX with an MCW H43/33F body which entered service in June 1972, swings around the bend as it descends the Bull Ring when working on the 50 route to the Maypole. The decline of the Bull Ring Centre and associated market area began as early as 1973. At the time when this 4226 was travelling out of the city centre, the Bull Ring complex was beginning to resemble a seedy, unloved and cheap-looking backwater, despite the prestigious nature of the centre when first opened in 1964. Behind the buses is St Martin's House, a glass-sided multi-storey office block opened in 1961 and designed by James A. Roberts, who was also responsible for the better-known Rotunda. The adjoining concrete car park had to be prematurely closed because of structural problems, although St Martin's House had a life of forty years surviving until late in 2001. (F.W. York)

The lined-out, pre-war livery, four-wheeled car 420 built in 1912 by UEC, is picking up passengers at the tram stop outside Morgan's sausage making and bacon curing premises near to Digbeth police station. The tram is working on the 42 route to Alcester Lanes End, King's Heath. Car 420 received its last repaint in September 1945 and survived until the last day of operation of the tram services on the Moseley Road route on 1 October 1949. Hidden by the tram is the Castle & Falcon public house on the corner of Meriden Street while the distant 1936 Morris Eight is about to pass the premises of the Digbeth branch of the Westminster Bank. (C. Carter)

A standard bus in the West Midlands PTE fleet was the MCW Metrobus MKII of which 688 examples were operational. Travelling into the city centre with only the destination blind showing the correct destination information is 2652 (ROX 652Y), a DR102/27 model which had entered service in June 1983. This picture dates from 22 November 1986, seven weeks after deregulation and the bus has already got West Midlands Travel fleet names. 2652 is crossing the Moat Row junction having just passed the exit to Digbeth Coach Station. (D.R. Harvey)

A careful examination of the overhead wiring in Digbeth shows only the positive tram wire in place. The buses working into the city in early 1953 are passing Jackson's tobacconist shop, well hidden by a plethora of advertisements. Leading the line of traffic is 1934 (HOV 934), an exposed-radiator Daimler CVD6 with a Metro-Cammell body which entered service on 1 October 1949. It is working on the 50B route from the old 42 tram terminus at Alcester Lanes End. Behind 1934 is a British Road Services Seddon 5L four-wheeled rigid lorry. This model weighed seven tons. The second bus is a 1948-vintage Daimler CVD6, 1838 (HOV 838), working on the 58C service from Wagon Lane, Sheldon. (D.R. Harvey collection)

Track repairs taking place in Digbeth on Sunday 19 May 1940 as bogie car 531 gingerly begins to negotiate the area under repair. It is travelling out of the city on the 42 route. In front of the tram is J. Gould's gentlemen's tailoring shop; he had taken over from his mother Mrs Rachel Gould during the 1930s. In the large building are the premises of Tomlinson the mill furnisher and through the archway is the iron merchant, Thomas Bonser. Behind the tramway track gang is the Digbeth shop of A.D. Wimbush. The handcart they are using is equipped with track-welding oxyacetylene bottles. (D. Clayton)

Daimler CVD6, 2063 (JOJ 63), a 'New-Look' front Metro-Cammell-bodied bus is working on the 50B route. Its driver, obviously trained by a former tram driver, has just dropped off a passenger, in the middle of the road, outside the Spencer House, an undistinguished 1950s office block which fronts Midland Red's Digbeth coach station. The sign for Wall's Ice Cream was less than common in Birmingham as the city was regarded as the territory of the Midland Counties Diary. The Old Bull's Head public house on the eastern side of Digbeth survived the road widening and redevelopment completed in July 1955 and is still a hostelry today. The distant five-storey Victorian factory block was occupied by H. Goodman who was a stencil cutter and engraver who also manufactured bronze, enamel and brass door plates. (D.R. Harvey collection)

The man carrying the paper bag is apparently unaware that behind him, a tram is coming round the bend from Digbeth into Rea Street. UEC-bodied, four-wheeled car 389 is on the 50 route to Trafalgar Road, the location of the tram depot. Although best known for air and oil brake cars like tram 436 (which is working on an inbound 42 service from Alcester Lanes End), there were usually about six of the 301 class kept at Moseley Road depot for duplicate and short workings on the main line along Moseley and Alcester Roads. Following tram 436, which is turning into Digbeth, with the Old Bull's Head public house and the Digbeth branch of Boots the Chemist on the opposite side of the road, is a Standard Little Nine saloon of 1932 vintage. (A.N. Porter)

The Digbeth end of Rea Street was very run down after years of planning blight and neglect. Rea Street ran alongside the River Rea which had a nearby fording point from before Domesday Book. The last bridge in Digbeth was built as recently as 1813, but in the late nineteenth century the river was channelled into a brick-lined culvert across both Digbeth and the distant Bradford Street. Midland Red had opened their bus garage in Rea Street on 3 January 1929 and by June 1958 Spencer House had replaced the open bus parking lot on the Digbeth frontage and the coach station was opened. Rea Street was used by trams, trolleybuses and latterly buses to link the Bradford Street and market area services with those in Digbeth. BCT 1940 (HOV 940), an exposed-radiator Daimler CVD6 travels into Birmingham in 1963 when working on the full-length 50 service from the Maypole. (D.R. Harvey collection)

Picking up passengers outside the old Fred Purkis' toy warehouse in Rea Street, opposite the entrance to the Birmingham Coach Station is West Midlands PTE, Park Royal-bodied Leyland Fleetline FE30AGR 6594 (NOC 594R). The Park Royal-bodied Fleetlines could be distinguished from the Metro-Cammell versions by the guttering over the emergency door of the former being shaped like a horizontal S, while the MCW version was an inverted U. The bus, which entered service in November 1976, is working on the 50 route, travelling away from Digbeth towards Bradford Street. The year is 1986 and the bus is proclaiming that the impending Conservative Government's transport bill, which would deregulate bus services, should be resisted. (D.R. Harvey)

UEC car 446 is travelling along Rea Street on an outbound 42 service to Alcester Lanes End in June 1949. The tram is about to turn left at the Belisha Crossing in front of the Premier Tyre Company shop on the corner of Bradford Street. The tram is being followed by a former military Bedford OYD truck. Weighing three tons, vehicles like this one were operational during the Second World War. Above the tram are the trolleybus wires used by the Coventry Road services which terminated in Station Street. (A. Yates)

The 50 route was a short working of the 42 route which terminated at Moseley Road depot and used the street crossover between the depot's two entrances to turn back. Car 425 turns out of Bradford Street into Rea Street in front of the large corner lantern of the Anchor Inn, a pub that in recent years has won numerous local CAMRA awards and a listing in their Real Ale Guide. On the opposite corner is the Premier Tyre Company shop while behind the tram is the interwar factory and warehouse occupied by a number of engineering companies. (Birmingham Central Reference Library)

Once the trams had turned into Bradford Street they crossed over the River Rea at the point of the culvert, before beginning the steep climb up to Moseley Road. Bradford Street had been a drover's route in the 1770s which accounted for its straightness and width. The street was named after one Henry Bradford who lived in Old Square and was a prominent Quaker, landlord and timber merchant in eighteenth-century Birmingham. Car 442, working into the city on a 42 service in 1949, has just crossed the culvert of the River Rea (though one would never know it) and passed the Premier Café, a name which seems a contradiction in terms. Behind 442 is the imposing factory of the Phosphor Bronze Company. (A. Yates)

3374 (374 KOV), an almost new Daimler Fleetline CRG6LX with a Metro-Cammell H44/33F body, was operating on the 50 route to the Maypole terminus at the city boundary on 4 August 1964. The bus had entered service on 6 July 1964. It is speeding up Bradford Street at Birchall Street which is

about halfway between Rea Street and Alcester Street. These buses at a stroke wiped out the exposed-radiator fleet of Daimler CVD6s (numbered 1931-1971) and transformed the Moseley Road services with their high seating capacity and front-loading platforms with power operated doors and heaters. Unfortunately many passengers disliked them from the start because they were poorly ventilated, had Vinyl plastic-covered seats and were bouncy to ride on. They were usually driven less than sympathetically by staff who had been seduced by the power of their 10.45-litre Gardner 6LX rear engines. The honeymoon period was therefore quite short! (Photofives)

On 22 November 1938, the tram wires which powered the trams travelling along Bradford Street are highlighted against the sky above the Alcester Street junction. The closure of the direct link from High Street, Bordesley to Camp Hill due to the abandonment of the Stratford Road group of tram routes on 5 January 1937 had an effect on the number of trams using Bradford Street. As well as being the route for the Moseley Road trams operating from Albert Street, Bradford Street now became the only way that trams could get to the overhaul and repair works at Kyotts Lake Road in Sparkbrook. On the left is the St Anne's Men's Club, with its strangely ecclesiastical windows while on the other side of Bradford Street, beyond the newly introduced Belisha Beacons is the already run-down, early nineteenth-century premises which so characterised this inner city part of Birmingham. Beyond the telephone box is the 1930s factory of confectioner Alfred Bird. (Birmingham Central Reference Library)

Turning out of Moseley Road and into the top of Bradford Street is totally enclosed car 726. These 702 class cars had their bodies assembled in 1925 at Moseley Road depot. The tram is travelling into the city centre on the 50 short working from the depot on 6 September 1949 and about to follow the speeding Austin 10hp car down the steep hill towards Rea Street. On the left is the Ansells-owned and very appropriately named Shepherd's Rest public house. These low-powered GEC 40hp trams were well suited to the steady, if unspectacular slogging of the Moseley Road group of routes. They operated until 2 April 1939, when, after the closure of the West Bromwich services, there was a large amount of tramcar redistribution and all thirty of the 32H class were moved to either Witton or Miller Street depot. Those 32H trams which survived the war returned to Moseley Road on 30 August 1947 for the last two years of tram operation. (G.F. Douglas)

On 18 August 1949, open-balcony, four-wheeled car 405, recently repainted in the 1946 livery with thin plain gold numbers travels out of the city and stands at the red request tram stop. About to turn left into Bradford Street is similarly repainted car 415, though this tram has managed to retain its pre-war shaded fleet name. Both trams are working on the 42 service. The tram stands alongside a row of very run-down three-storey mid-Victorian properties, with embellishments of entablatures and architraves falsely suggesting that the properties facing the road were better than those in the courtyards. On the north side of Bradford Street is the 1920s building which was the Adam & Eve public house in Warner Street. (A.N.H. Glover)

This was the grim, run-down squalor of the three-storey back-to-back homes which lined Moseley Road. The entries, alternating with front doors, usually led to a typically blue-bricked courtyard with a wash-house, a communal lavatory block and originally just one water pump. On the left is Mrs Rebecca Johnson's greengrocery which was the first retail outlet in Moseley Road, while just behind the parked Oxford-registered 1937 Wolseley Series II 25 hp saloon is a bus stop, in place for the impending conversion of the route to buses. Car 415, working on an outbound 42 service, picks up passengers who have to walk across the Moseley Road cobbles in order to get onto their tram. (R.T. Wilson)

Alexander-bodied Scania N113DR, 3229 (H229 LOM), belonging to West Midlands Travel, is working on the 50 route to the Maypole. These buses were bought to replace some Mark I Metrobuses and became the workhorses on the Moseley Road for about nine years. The Scanias could always be recognised, even when out of sight, as when hot, their brakes squealed very loudly and could often be heard over a mile away! 3229 is travelling out of Birmingham in Moseley Road in August 1993, about to pass the entrance to Highgate Park. The 8.4-acre park was opened on 2 June 1876 and despite being extensively bombed during the Second World War, survived as an oasis of greenery amidst an inner city landscape. By 1993, this part of Moseley Road was still being used for a mixture of industrial and residential purposes, but the mid and late nineteenth-century buildings, with the exception of a few public houses, have largely disappeared and been replaced by low-rise flats and offices. (D.R. Harvey)

3363 (363 KOV), has just passed Stratford Place on its way into the city centre on a 50K service from Alcester Lanes End in June 1964 when the bus was brand new and its paintwork positively sparkling. Behind the bus are some classically styled suburban villas which were built in the late eighteenth and early nineteenth centuries when this part of Balsall Heath was identified as a 'genteel neighbourhood'. Within a few years lands owned by the Moore and Edwards families were quickly sold off for housing in increasingly small lots so that even these good-quality houses were sitting cheek by jowl with artisan terraces, back-to-backs and unhygienic courtyards. (A.B. Cross)

Birmingham Central Tramways opened its Moseley Road and Balsall Heath steam tram routes as far as Moseley Village on 29 December 1884. Constructed on 3ft 6in. gauge, this was one of eight routes which CBT opened with steam trams. From 1887 the route was extended to King's Heath and this situation continued until New Year's Eve 1906 when the twenty-one-year lease expired and the operation was transferred to the municipally-owned Birmingham Corporation Tramways. The electric overhead is already in place as this Falcon seven-window steam tram pulls a Falcon trailer from Moseley Village, passing by Highgate Park on the cold, snowy day when steam tram operation ceased. The steam tram has just passed Stratford House which was built in 1601 for Ambrose Rotton as a farmhouse for the estimated twenty acres of farmland, between the Moseley and Stratford Roads that belonged to him. With its timber frames, the building is a typical seventeenth-century Warwickshire farmhouse. (J. Whybrow collection)

Belgrave Middleway was completed in the 1970s and although the main route of the A4540 Middleway turned north-east on Highgate Middleway, a short new section following the original line of Belgrave

Road was built to the Moseley Road junction at Highgate Road. On this 200-yard section of road all the old buildings were swept away, leaving a windswept expanse on the steep hill leading off Moseley Road. Inbound buses used this section of road before turning up Highgate Middleway and rejoining Moseley Road near to Highgate Park. Alexander-bodied Scania N113DR, 3224 (H224 LOM), entered service from Birmingham Central garage, in September 1990 and in April 1991 is working on the 50 route as a Ford Transit van speeds up the hill towards the Moseley Road traffic lights. (D.R. Harvey)

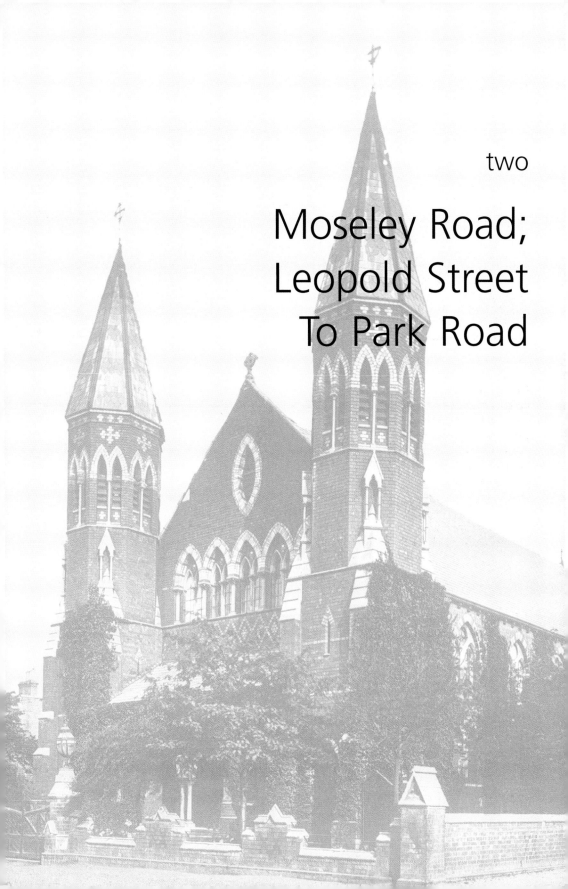

two

Moseley Road;
Leopold Street
To Park Road

If there was a type of tram which characterised the Moseley Road services it was the fifty members of the 401 class which arrived between August 1912 and March 1913. They entered service, working with only their hand and rheostatic brakes, at peak periods from Bournbrook and Miller Street depots. It was only after the autumn of 1913 that they were equipped with the Spencer-Dawson air and oil brakes and transferred to Moseley Road depot to operate on the steep incline of the Leopold Street service. Car 438 travels along Moseley Road on an inbound 42 route on 24 July 1949. It is negotiating the track work at the Leopold Street junction. In the distance is the Alhambra Cinema which opened on Boxing Day 1928 and closed as the ABC Moseley Road on 31 August 1968. On this summer's day in 1949 the cinema was showing *Dear Octopus* with Margaret Lockwood and *Tower of London* starring Boris Karloff, Basil Rathbone and Vincent Price. (A.D. Packer)

It is Sunday 26 March 1939 as tram 725 approaches the left turn which will take it into Leopold Street on the 51 service from Alcester Lanes End to Hill Street. Mrs Sarah Gibbs's newsagent shop appears to be closed though she has kept her notice boards outside, one proclaiming that a new *Saint* story by

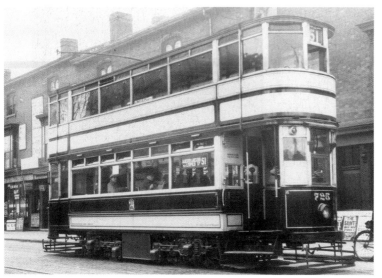

Leslie Charteris is to appear in the long-forgotten *Empire News*. Car 725 was one of thirty totally enclosed, sixty-three-seater cars delivered by Brush at the end of 1925. They were fitted with GEC WH32H 40hp motors and although a trifle slow on gradients such as Leopold Street, gave good service, with the exception of those destroyed during the war, until their withdrawal in July 1953. (L.W. Perkins)

1671, (HOV 671), a Brush-bodied Leyland Titan PD2/1, which had entered service with BCT on 1 October 1948, is working on an inbound 35 service from the Maypole to Station Street alongside New Street Station. The 35 route, introduced originally as the cross-city 17 service to Erdington on 19 March 1928, was operated by Yardley Wood garage after 1938, so for about one year these handsome vehicles were a familiar sight along Moseley and Alcester Roads. When the Moseley Road tram routes were closed on 1 October 1949, the 35 bus service went with them. On the right is the Society of Friends' Hall and Institute, known latterly as the Moseley Road Institute. This was opened in 1899 having been paid for by Richard Cadbury, whose family had already set up pioneering Adult Education classes in Stirchley for the workers of the Bournville chocolate factory. Designed by Ewen Harper, it had a large galleried hall with a seating capacity for 2,000, a smaller hall for 400 and some thirty-seven classrooms. (D.R. Harvey collection)

Camp Hill and Balsall Heath Station was originally opened by the Birmingham and Gloucester Railway on 17 December 1840 on their way towards their intended Curzon Street terminus which they shared with the London and Birmingham Railway after 17 August in the following year. This suburban station was closed as a Second World War economy measure on 27 January 1941 along with Brighton Road, Moseley and King's Heath stations. All of these stations were permanently closed on 27 November 1946. A number of passengers and the stationmaster stand at the Birmingham end of the platforms in July 1906 with the houses on Highgate Road on either side of the railway bridge. (R.S. Carpenter)

The Midland Railway had followed the policy of having small locomotives and short trains throughout the latter years of the nineteenth century, but when Richard Mountford Deeley became Chief Mechanical Engineer in 1904 he soon addressed this problem and in 1907 introduced a class of forty 0-6-4T suburban passenger locomotives. Deeley's 'Hole-the-Wall' or 'Flat Iron' tanks were principally employed in the areas of Birmingham and South East Lancashire and with a tractive effort of 19,756lbs and 5ft 7in. driving wheels they were well suited to the fast starts required on suburban stop-start local services. LMS 2003 drifts southwards through Camp Hill Station when working 'light' and southwards on 21 February 1936. The whole class were fitted with Belpaire Fireboxes and superheated during the early 1920s, but all were withdrawn between 1935 and 1938 when their boilers had worn out and the more powerful, stable and efficient 2-6-4T were introduced. (A.N.H. Glover)

The junction of Moseley Road and Highgate Road was adjacent to Camp Hill Station and behind the buildings on the right was a widening fan of railway tracks which went as far as Stratford Place. In 1880, the state of the roads generally was appalling, with mud and horse manure making them look more like a Wild West main street than Balsall Heath. This would change dramatically four years later when the Birmingham Central Tramway began its operation of steam trams along Moseley Road. Soon the purported 1840s shops of Highgate House would be replaced by a suitably imposing building for the Midland Bank, while, coincidentally, the Highgate Tea Mart grocery shop premises on the corner of Montpellier Street would also be replaced by a bank, in this case owned by Lloyds. (Birmingham Central Reference Library)

Travelling along Moseley Road when approaching the Belgrave Road junction is Volvo B7TL 4251 (BU 51 RVJ). This bus had an Alexander H47/27F body and is working into the city on 25 May 2002, when it was just seven months old. The bus has been branded for the 50 route. These Volvos replaced the Scanias of 1991 as the main Travel West Midlands buses on the Moseley Road services. (D.R. Harvey)

Speeding along the tree-lined Moseley Road approaching Belgrave Road on its way into the city is a brand-new Metro-Cammell-bodied Daimler Fleetline 3370 (370 KOV), still being worked by a two-man crew. It has just passed the bay-windowed Victorian house which was being used as the headquarters of the 41st Sea Cadets. It will shortly reach the traffic lights where the Inner Circle 8 bus route crossed Moseley Road. (A.B. Cross)

Standing at the compulsory stop outside the terrace of 1840s houses in Moseley Road is UEC four-wheeled tram 443. It is in full post-war livery having been repainted as recently as 6 February 1948. The 443 was one of thirty-seven open-balcony trams to remain in all-day service for the next thirty-six years until the abandonment of the Moseley Road group of routes on 1 October 1949. Opposite the tram is the Moseley Picture House with its pavement canopy. Opened on 12 May 1913, this was one of the earliest suburban cinemas in Birmingham. It was finally demolished in 1974 as part of the Belgrave Middleway road-widening scheme. The large building with the cupola beyond the cinema is the impressive Belgrave Hotel, built in 1878, which overlooked the Moseley Road and Belgrave Road junction. (A.N.H. Glover)

A UEC-bodied open-balcony four-wheeled tram, car 415 stands in Moseley Road at the junction with Vincent Street. On the corner, behind the tram is the long-established confectionery and tobacconist's shop of Thomas Sparrow, which is advertising traditional St Bruno pipe tobacco and has an early type of vending machine for Beech Nut chewing gum. It is 9 September 1939 and car 415 has been fitted

with the first type of ARP headlight hood. Its edgings and steps have also been painted white so that, in the total darkness of the blackout, passengers had a small clue as to where the vehicle ended and the road began. (L.W. Perkins)

Mr Fred Butler stands besides his Shell petrol pumps and watches two girls alight from car 424. This tram is working on the 42 route along Moseley Road on its way out of the city on 10 September 1949. In front of the tram, the 1935 Coventry-registered Morris Twelve has been carefully parked so that it does not obstruct the tram tracks. The adult entertainments to be found in this part of Moseley Road included the

Billiard and Snooker Social Club above the shop on the extreme right and the Castle and Dragon public house. On this sunny autumn day, more open-air pleasures are to be enjoyed by the young children and their father as they ride on the balcony of the tram. This was something which they could only savour for another three weeks before the closure of the tram route. The Moseley Road group of services were the last 3ft 6in gauge tram routes to be operated by open-balcony four-wheeled trams in the United Kingdom. (A.N.H. Glover)

In 1862, Balsall Heath obtained Urban District status, with an urban population of 10,000 people crammed into some ten miles of streets. In the thirty years after 1862, Balsall Heath had become a honey pot of industrial development and had its own school board, a hospital, and water and sewage management schemes. Yet in 1891, Balsall Heath was taken over by its big brother, much to the annoyance of the local population. The Free Library in Moseley Road, designed by J.H. Cossins & Peacock, was opened in 1896 and built alongside the Art Nouveau-fronted swimming baths. The Free Library is housed in the building on the left with three decorative gables while the baths are next to the little cart which is parked beneath the trees. Open-balcony car 418 travels into Birmingham on the 42 service in the summer of 1921. (D.R. Harvey collection)

The interior of the Edwardian Balsall Heath swimming baths was a symphony in polished tiling and wrought iron. The opening by the Lord Mayor of Birmingham on 30 October 1907 had been delayed because the aquifer level in the artesian well for the bath's water supply was at a depth of 727ft and took several years to reach! This splendid building, designed by architect W. Hale, had a first class swimming baths which has a spectator's gallery, the second class swimming pool (pictured here), first and second class men's and women's private baths, a clubroom and a small laundry. Although a Grade II Listed Building, as well as being the last surviving washing baths in Birmingham, this wonderful building is in a poor state of repair and was closed in 2005 with funding of an estimated £15 million required to restore them to their former glory. (Birmingham Central Reference Library)

St Paul's Church was unusually first mooted in the Wagon and Horses public house by seven gentlemen during May 1850. It was built to the designs of J.L. Pedley on the corner of St Paul's Road in the decorative Gothic style of the Victorian Age, with seating for over 1,100 worshippers. This large church, consecrated in 1853, with its massive embattled west tower, had alongside the nave, a large southern aisle and a chancel. The church was closed in 1980 and moved to the Church Centre in Edward Road. (Birmingham Central Reference Library)

The School of Art in Moseley Road was built in 1899 for artistically talented secondary school pupils. This two-storey, red brick and stone building was designed by W.H. Bidlake with a distinctive round arched decorative gable and a two-storey stone portico. The school held a reputable position in the teaching of arts and crafts, particularly for use in Birmingham's many industries, until it closed in 1975. The last all-electric tram purchased by Birmingham Corporation was car 731 of which the Brush-body was assembled at Moseley Road depot in January 1926. It is not actually working a 39 service but has come up Edward Road on the left from Balsall Heath and is going to travel forward to the next crossover before working empty back to the depot at Trafalgar Road. (R.T. Wilson)

The unique tram 431 had been used as a single-deck tractor unit between 1916 and 1922 on the Nechells route. When converted to double-deck it received a covered top (built at Kyotts Lake Road) which did not have window vents. The tram received a 'light touch-up' on 17 November 1945 in the pre-war livery style and is carrying an advertisement for Keiller's Dundee Marmalade which was first made in 1797 when a Spanish ship carrying Seville oranges took refuge in Dundee's harbour. A local grocer by the name of James Keiller purchased the cargo and his wife Janet boiled the oranges with sugar and made, for the first time, orange marmalade. The tram is passing the New Imperial Picture House which was located on the corner of Clifton Road. It is showing the 1948 film *Whispering Smith* starring Alan Ladd as a western railway detective, with co-stars Robert Preston and Brenda Marshall. (R.F. Mack)

The Congregational Church on the corner of Runcorn Road was a readily visible landmark as it had twin west end spires which were covered with a distinct lining. The church opened in 1862 with seating for about 1,000 people. During the Second World War, the crypt was used as an air-raid shelter. The church was demolished in the 1960s having not been used for some years. (Birmingham Central Reference Library)

An as yet unadorned Alexander-bodied Volvo B7LE 4244 (BU 51 RUR), passes the row of 1990s buildings on the corner of Brighton Road as it drives through the traffic lights. The bus, which had only entered service in October 2001, is travelling towards Moseley Village on the 50 route on 15 January 2002. (D.R. Harvey)

Cromer Road dates from the last twenty years of the nineteenth century and contained a strange mixture of good-quality Victorian villas as well as terraces of more artisan-like dwellings. The tall building beyond the lady pedestrian is Tindal Street Junior and Infant School which opened in 1880 with a capacity of initially just over 800 children. On the right, in Cromer Road, is Brighton Road post office whose address was confusingly, 577 Moseley Road. At one time, behind the trees, was a long-neglected, rather fancy and bogusly-named mansion called the Priory which had been occupied in the nineteenth century by John Cartland, a Birmingham brass founder. Wednesday 18 June 1924 must have been a rather quiet day as there is hardly any vehicular traffic, though there is a lady waiting for a tram to arrive from Moseley. (Birmingham Central Reference Library)

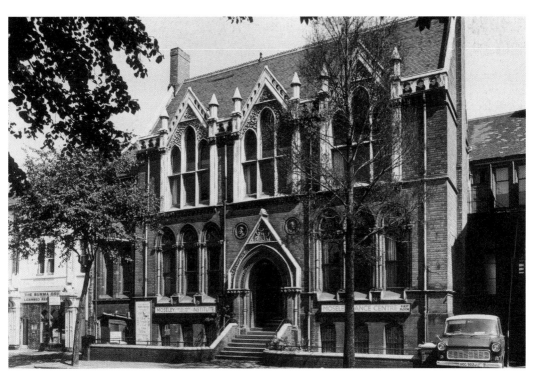

The Moseley and Balsall Heath Institute was built in 1883 by John Bowen and designed in a pseudo-ecclesiastical, Gothic style. It had a central entrance with an arched and decorated head which is approached by climbing a short flight of steps. The building, despite its size, is only two storeys high though it has a large sub-basement. The origin of the Institute was the Mechanics Institute whose aim was the self-improvement of Victorian artisans and the courses were initiated by the Cadbury Brothers at Bournville. In 1906, Moseley Road tram depot was built next door. (Birmingham Central Reference Library)

Standing outside the Moseley and Balsall Heath Institute is UEC-built car 405. The northern entrance, triangle tracks into Moseley Road depot are visible beneath and in front of the tram. The tram is working on the 42 route to Alcester Lanes End but has only attracted one lady passenger. On the left is the waste ground which had been the former site of the nineteenth-century priory while on the opposite side of the Cromer Road traffic lights is the Brighton Road post office. (F.N. Lloyd Jones)

The grounds of the old priory opposite Moseley Road tram depot were used as a bus parking lot immediately after the abandonment of the Moseley Road tram services. This was because as a tram depot the capacity was about 80 trams; the number of replacement buses was virtually the same and there was insufficient room to break up the nine 301 class cars and all the thirty-eight remaining 401 class cars. Pictured here are at least twenty buses in the yard, six of which are the new 1931-1972 allocation of exposed-radiator Daimler CVD6s. (G.F. Douglas)

Travelling into Birmingham on 3 March 1972 is a West Midlands PTE bus working on the 49F short working from Moseley Village to Suffolk Street. This bus route had replaced the 65 tram service on 1 October 1949. 4175 (YOX 175K) was a Daimler Fleetline CRG6LX with a MCW H43/33F body which had entered service during the previous month from Moseley Road garage which is behind the bus and scheduled to close in just two days. Travelling in the other direction is a Guy Big J 7-ton lorry. (D.R. Harvey Collection)

On the last day of Moseley Road's tram services, car 729, an EMB bogie Brush-bodied sixty-three-seater, totally enclosed tram of 1926 vintage, stands outside the depot. It was working on the 41 service from Navigation Street to Trafalgar Road, which was alongside the depot. Its trolley pole has already been turned for the return journey by way of Leopold Street. On the following day, car 729 would leave Moseley Road depot and be transferred to Miller Street where it would work on the Erdington group of services until the final day of Birmingham's tram operations. (D.R. Harvey Collection)

On a sunny summer's day in 1950, two of the pre-war buses which augmented the new replacement buses introduced on 2 October 1949, stand outside Moseley Road garage while crew members begin and end their duties. The leading bus working to the Maypole on a 50 service is 1129 (CVP 229). This is a Daimler COG5 with a Metro-Cammell H30/24R body which had entered service on 15 November 1937 and would remain in service until New Year's Eve 1960. Behind is an equally dusty-looking 993 (COX 993), which entered service on 1 June 1937 and is working to Alcester Lanes End on the 48B route. This bus finished its career as a snowplough from November 1954 until July 1963. (S.N.J. White)

Moseley Road tram depot, also referred to as Trafalgar Road depot, was opened on 1 January 1907 with an allocation believed to be of the first twenty-five of the 71-220 class of UEC-bodied Radial trucked four-wheelers. The depot was extended during 1912 and by January 1914, all of the 401 class trams, which were then less than eighteen months old, had been fitted with Spencer-Dawson air and oil brakes and were working on Moseley Road. They would remain as the backbone of the Moseley Road tram routes for the next thirty-six years. Near to the end of its life, car 424 stands on the depot forecourt alongside a sign which would send modern day Health and Safety officials into a state of apoplexy! (D.R. Harvey collection)

The view into Moseley Road garage in 1959 shows lines of sparkling buses waiting for their next duties. Visible are the three types of buses, all with fifty-four-seater Metro-Cammell bodies, operated by the garage at this time. These were the exposed-radiator 1949-built Daimler CVD6s of the 1931 class of which bus 1946, (HOV 946), is on the extreme left along with another unidentifiable one. On the right is 2046 (JOJ 46), a Daimler CVD6 with a concealed 'New-Look' radiator. In the centre is 1055 (CVP 155), a 1937 Daimler COG5 which was one of forty-one brought out of the store in 1958 for two years to augment the bus fleet when the Walsall and College Road services were taken over from Midland Red. (R.F. Mack/F.W. York)

Preparatory to the evening peak period and in order to expedite the buses' quick entry into service, Moseley Road frequently used to park buses alongside the garage in Trafalgar Road. Birmingham was unusual in that during the day only about thirty percent of the fleet was in service, but during the morning and evening peaks over ninety percent of the buses would be out on the road leaving the garages empty except for buses undergoing repairs. Bus 1101 (CVP 201), a 1937 Metro-Cammell-bodied Daimler COG5, stands in Trafalgar Road on 22 May 1950 prior to working up and down Leopold Street on the 49A route. (L.W. Perkins)

A Travel West Midlands Scania N113DRB with an Alexander H45/31F body, 3247, (H247 LOM), which entered service in November 1990, heads past the frontage of the old Moseley Road tram depot and subsequent bus garage. 3274 is working on the 50 route along Moseley Road on the 11 March 1996 and is going to the Druids Heath housing development. (D.R. Harvey)

Moseley Road bus garage, on the corner of Trafalgar Road, closed on 5 March 1972, when all bus operation was transferred to Liverpool Street garage. It was sold on 15 February 1975 and has had various uses including being used as a go-carting track and a skateboard centre. Some twenty-nine years later it is having some restoration work undertaken on its Grade II frontage. Bus 58 (J58 GCX), speeds along Moseley Road towards Moseley Village. This five-year old DAF SB220 with an Ikarus B50F body was new to Smiths of Shenington, as their low cost Your Bus operation, was working on their 50Y service to the Druids Heath terminus of West Midlands Travel. (D.R. Harvey)

'The king is dead, long live the king!' Shown here are four brand-new Metro-Cammell-bodied Daimler Fleetline CRG6LX buses which had been placed into service during June and July 1964. The only identifiable bus is 2052 (JOJ 52), a 'New-Look' front Daimler CVD6 which is travelling along Alcester Road towards Trafalgar Road on a 49 service from King's Heath into the city via Leopold Street in July 1964. This bus entered service on 1 December 1950 June and was withdrawn on 31 January 1966. These CVD6 buses ran alongside the new Fleetlines for only about eighteen months. (D.R. Harvey collection)

This section of Alcester Road climbing from the edge of Balsall Heath up the hill to the Alcester Road turnpike tollhouse on the corner of Park Road was developed during the early years of Queen Victoria's reign. This Balsall Heath and Moseley boundary area was once forested, being cleared as early as 1772 but remaining as a common until the heathland was built over after about 1840. Car 443 has left the distant Trafalgar Road when working out of the city on the 42 route and is travelling towards Moseley Village. It has just passed (seen behind the trees on the right) the incredibly narrow Louise Lorne Street and the impressive Brighton Place terrace built in 1855. (F.N. Lloyd Jones)

A Falcon 0-4-0 steam locomotive, number 53, dating from 1886, hauls its Falcon double-ended, sixty-seat trailer with seven side windows up Alcester Road towards Moseley Village. The steam tram is letting out some smoke from its chimney which was strictly speaking prohibited by the Board of Trade Regulations, but which was nearly impossible to prevent, even with all the condensation tubes on the roof of the locomotive. The trailer is carrying the letter 'M' showing that the tram is going to the terminus at Institute Road, King's Heath although the slip-board states that it is going only as far as Moseley. (D.R. Harvey collection)

The large house at the junction of Alcester Road and Park Road where the main A435 becomes Alcester Road was demolished in the 1980s and replaced by blocks of low-rise luxury flats. On 10 December 1997, 3234 (H234 LOM), is about to cross from Moseley Road and go into Alcester Road as it approaches Moseley when working on the 50 route to Druids Heath. (D.R. Harvey)

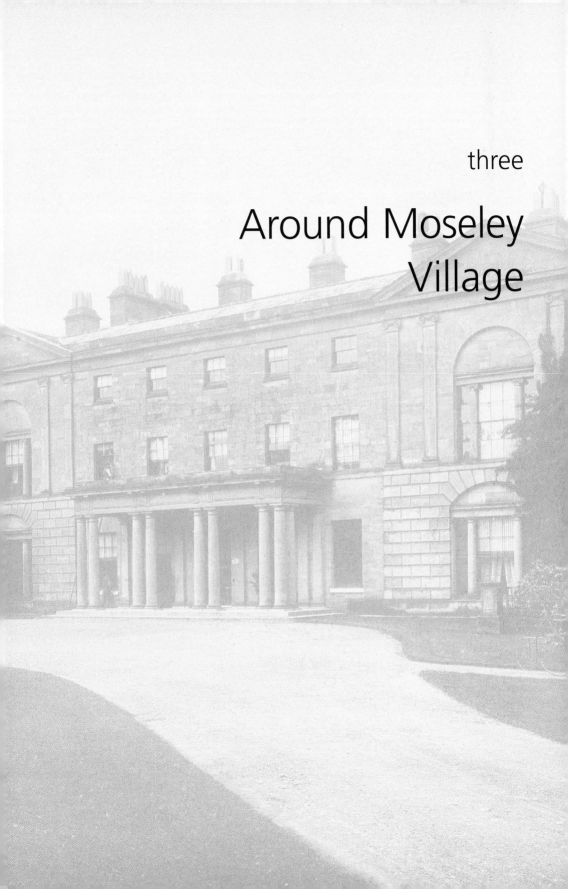

three

Around Moseley Village

Park Road was laid out in 1865 and the upper end had villas in eclectic styles of no distinction. Hidden through the trees between the two trams was a large house standing in the angle of Alcester Road and Park Road. On the left is the location of where the 1766 tollhouse and gate on the Alcester turnpike stood. Car 418 is travelling along Alcester Road on an inbound 42 service to Albert Street on 9 August 1947. It is being overtaken by 1228 (FOF 228), a 1939 MCCW-bodied Daimler COG5 which is working on the express service 35 into the somewhat out-of-the-way city terminus in Station Street. Waiting for the traffic to pass at the top of Park Road is car 429 which is working on an outbound 39. (J.H. Tayleforth collection)

In Alcester Road approaching Moseley Village in 1949 is car 387, one of the hundred strong 301 class which entered service around the cusp of 1911 and 1912. It has just come out of Park Road when working on an outbound 39 service. It is passing the splendid 1930s-style petrol pumps at the Ashfield Motors garage, which are dispensing Shell and Esso petrol as well as the long-forgotten Cleveland petrol brand whose illuminated pump sign was triangular. Although not fitted with the air and oil brake, car 387 had been at Moseley Road depot as one of just four of the class since January 1945. (D.R. Harvey Collection)

In about 1909, two of the still almost new Radial cars, 81 on the left and 71 on the right, pass each other in Alcester Road. Both of these top-covered trams are in their 'as delivered' condition with open vestibules which left their drivers exposed to the elements. Beyond the two tram cars is Park Hill. On the extreme left is the early nineteenth-century Prince of Wales public house, while opposite are the large late Victorian residential villas which had been built along this section of Alcester Road. (Commercial Postcard)

The early nineteenth-century Prince of Wales public house in Alcester Road really marked the northern limit of Moseley Village. Towards the end of the nineteenth century, when the the staff of the pub are pictured standing outside the Georgian building, CBT steam tram service was in operation. The visible

windows on the ground floor of the Prince of Wales are fitted with wooden Venetian blinds, while the other floors have canvas ones. The landlord at the time was one William Haynes who was licensed to sell beer, ale and porter (which was brewed by Holts), as well as dealing in tobacco. The typically large lamp over the pub's entrance advertises wines and spirits. (Birmingham Central Reference Library)

The initial allocation of Corporation trams to Mosley Road depot on 1 January 1907 consisted of about twenty-five of the first vehicles from the 71-220 class of UEC-bodied trams. Car 81, equipped with flop-over destination boards rather than the early vestibule-mounted destination box, is travelling towards the city from Alcester Lanes End through Moseley Village in about 1910. There were 150 of these 71 class trams whose M&G 8ft 6in Radial trucks were quickly known for their rough riding qualities and were later replaced. The recently constructed Edwardian retail premises with their steep gables provided the residents with a wide range of shops, while the horse drawn cart of Lansdown's Laundry is parked outside the mock Tudor-cum-Arts and Crafts design premises of W H Smith, the already nationwide news agency. (Commercial Postcard)

Moseley Station, seen on 22 July 1929, was not opened until 1867. Its quaint single-storey Midland Railway-style station buildings were built deep in the cutting and reached by ramps from St Mary's Row and Blayney Street. Because of the timber bridge by which Blayney Street crossed the cutting it was

renamed Woodbridge Road. Few trains stopped at Moseley initially, but after 1875 when Brighton Road Station was opened, there was a choice of thirty trains a day to New Street. The station was closed by the LMS as a wartime economy effort on 27 January 1941. Through the strangely Gothic-inspired tunnel beneath St Mary's Row, the tracks ran on towards Kings Norton. (R.S. Carpenter)

Muselei was first mentioned in the Domesday Book meaning 'an open grassy area with some trees, (*leah*), which was infested by mice'. Moseley's old village green at the wide-throated junction of St Mary's Row and Alcester Road was the first place to be urbanised. The buildings on the south side were completed in the early 1880s before the steam trams reached Moseley. In about 1895, three hansom cabs stand alongside the steam tram tracks which encircled the green and in front of the cab men's hut. They are facing up the hill towards the parish church of St Mary. This church, dating from 1780, is hidden by the Shoeing Forge and the Miles' cab and car yard beneath the archway extension to the recently rebuilt Bull's Head public house. (Birmingham Central Reference Library)

The driver of the City of Birmingham Tramways Company Falcon steam locomotive has turned his vehicle into St Mary's Row when pulling trailer 56, a Falcon double-ended sixty-seater bogie car. The steam tram would uncouple from the trailer, run around St Mary's Row loop and if necessary obtain water and coke before re-coupling to the other end of the trailer. Behind the tram is the open land which was part of Moseley Park. By 1902, the Victoria Parade row of shops had been completed. (D.R. Harvey collection)

The CBT steam tram is on its way to King's Heath in about 1904. It is about to pass Mr Eade's horse and cart which is plodding past the entrance to St Mary's Row. To the right of the tram on the corner of King Edward's Road is the impressive terracotta Fighting Cocks Hotel which had been built in 1899 by the Holt Brewery with two smoke rooms and an L-shaped bar. As part of the rebuilding of the original inn, the brewery had to build the adjacent shops at an additional cost of £6,000. On the left is the Victoria Parade row of shops which by this date were well established. (Commercial postcard)

On a hot summer's day in about 1909, the three-year old UEC-bodied, fifty-two-seat tramcar 91 loads up with passengers in Alcester Road, Moseley Village. Behind the tram is the Fighting Cocks row of buildings including the public house with its impressive clock tower. The car is fitted with flop-over destination boards and is on its way out of Birmingham on the King's Heath service from Hill Street via Leopold Street. On the right behind the policeman is the triangle of land at the bottom of St Mary's Row, though by this date, the steam tracks around the loop had been removed. (Commercial postcard)

One of the focal points of Moseley Village is the splendid terracotta-detailed Fighting Cocks which was built by the Holts Brewery in 1899 at the substantial cost of £4,000. It was designed by the architects Newton and Cheatle and unusually incorporated into the design was a barometer which reflected the interest in meteorology of one of the brewery's directors. Parked in front of this Grade II Listed public house in St Mary's Row about 1959, are two exposed-radiator Daimler CVD6s. The vehicle numbered 1947 (HOV 947) is changing crew on its way to the Maypole on the 48 route. Behind it is bus 1962 (HOV 962), which is at its Moseley terminus having worked on the 49 service via Leopold Street. (A.D. Broughall)

Moseley Village centre has changed remarkably little since its completion around the beginning of the twentieth century. On a sunny spring day in April 1992, the multi-gabled Victoria Parade of shops on the left has the Moseley branch of Boots the Chemist located on the corner of Salisbury Road. On the right the Art Nouveau-style Fighting Cocks pub and the row of shops going into St Mary's Row are still substantially the same. The bus waiting at the traffic lights is the Alexander-bodied Scania N113DR 3208 (H208 LOM), which is on its way to the Druids Heath terminus of the 50 service located at the Maypole Estate. (D.R. Harvey)

Turning out of Salisbury Road in about 1950 on a 48B service to Alcester Lanes End is bus 1938 (HOV 938), a Daimler CVD6 with a Metro-Cammell body. Following it is an unidentified Metro-Cammell-bodied Daimler COG5 of 1937 vintage. Between the buses, the Salisbury Road corner property of the Victoria Parade shops is occupied by Boots the Chemist. Salisbury Road, named after Queen Victoria's last prime minister, was cut through the grounds of Moseley Hall and finally gained access from Edgbaston Road in 1899, which is notable for its good-quality Arts and Crafts houses. The parked car in the foreground is an April 1947-registered Rover Twelve Sports saloon. (D.R. Harvey collection)

The eighteenth-century premises of Bullock and Hooper stood on Alcester Road on Welsh's Hill going out of Moseley Village towards King's Heath. This old row of cottages, which were still occupied in the early 1880s, would be cleared as part of the cutting of Salisbury Road which began in 1896. As yet there are no steam tram tracks. These would be laid later for the opening of the extension to King's Heath on 1 February 1887. A coke yard for the CBT steam trams was opened in a yard on the left and if the tram locomotives required raking out it was here that they came. (Birmingham Central Reference Library)

Partly hidden by the bus is the eighteenth-century, brick-built octagonal Dovecote which was one of the outbuildings of Moseley Hall. The bus 3243 (H243 LOM), is a Scania N113DR with a seventy-six-seat Alexander body which entered service in November 1990. It is travelling down the hill from Reddings Road and approaching Moseley Village on the 50 route in April 1991. (D.R. Harvey)

The core of the present Moseley Hall Hospital was the Georgian building, Moseley Hall which stood between Moseley Village and Reddings Road. This was rebuilt between 1792 and 1796 to the designs of John Standbridge of Warwick after being sacked in the Priestley Riots of 1791. This happened at a time when the hall was owned by the Taylor family who were wealthy button manufacturers from Bordesley. By 1884 the house was bought by Richard Cadbury (one of the chocolate-making family) who subsequently gave the house to the Birmingham Corporation on the proviso that it would be used as a children's convalescent home. (Birmingham Central Reference Library)

Very occasionally, a Birmingham bus would have something wrong with it when in service. In this case the number blinds have become tangled in the rollers although the destination wording shows that the bus is working on route 50B to the turning circle adjacent to King's Heath dog track. Bus 2045 (JOJ 45), a 'New-Look' front Daimler CVD6 is climbing Welsh's Hill and, having just passed the entrance to Moseley Hall Hospital, is approaching the junction with Reddings Road where Moseley RFC played at their Reddings ground from 1880 until 2000. (PM Photography)

The tram travelling into Birmingham on rthe 42 route is car 389, a 1912-built UEC tram mounted on UEC swing-yoke 7ft 6in. trucks and powered by 40hp motors. As these four-wheelers were not fitted with extra braking as per class 401, they were not allowed to operate on the Leopold Street turns. Tram 389 has climbed up the hill in Alcester Road from the Queensbridge Road junction and is passing the large, typical Moseley Arts and Crafts villas dating from just before the end of Queen Victoria's reign. This tram had been at the Coventry Road depot until December 1944 and remained as one of the seven trams of class 301 to survive until the closure of the Moseley Road routes. (F.N. Lloyd Jones)

Decorated in the post-war livery that it had been given in January 1947, open-balcony four-wheeled car 402 is negotiating the traffic island at the junction with Queensbridge Road. Interestingly, the motor traffic went around the island on both sides, but the trams, irrespective of their direction, went around only one side of the island. The tram is travelling towards King's Heath working on service 42 to Alcester Lanes End. Behind the distant tram at the top of the hill are the Arts and Crafts villas shown in the previous photograph. (F.N. Lloyd Jones)

Highbury Hall was designed by the Birmingham architect J.H. Chamberlain as a large Victorian suburban house for Joseph Chamberlain, the name being a pure coincidence! When construction was first begun in 1878, the site of Highbury Hall was in open country between Moseley, Edgbaston and King's Heath. The resulting magnificent family home used granite, brick, plaster and iron on the outside while within, wood panelling and tiles were the order of the day. It was named 'Highbury' after the area in north London from which Joseph Chamberlain's family hailed. (Birmingham Central Reference Library)

Facing Camp Hill in about 1910, King's Heath Station was suitably devoid of railway traffic although the picture shows a few possible passengers congregating between the footbridge and the signal box located at the north end of the down platform. King's Heath Station was opened by the Birmingham and Gloucester Railway on 17 December 1840 as Moseley Station but was renamed 'King's Heath' by the Midland Railway on 1 November 1867. The distant High Street road bridge can be seen beyond the footbridge. The single-storey, gabled buildings are typical of Midland Railway style. Access to the station could be gained down a drive from High Street. The station was closed for passenger traffic on 27 January 1941. (Lens of Sutton)

King's Heath Station was still served by freight trains until the 'Beeching Axe' and it was still being used for this purpose on 22 October 1962. This is when bus 2045 (JOJ 45), a Daimler CVD6 with a Metro–Cammell H30/24R body was travelling away from High Street, King's Heath, towards Queensbridge Road when working on the 48 route. Parked alongside the advertising hoardings are a 1956 Morris Oxford II, an Austin A55 Cambridge and an Austin A99 Westminster. (D.R. Harvey collection)

four

Through King's
Heath

High Street, Kings Heath

Picking up passengers on the corner of Station Road is tramcar 102, built in 1907. The tram is on its way to Hill Street from King's Heath in about 1910. Behind the tram is the entrance drive to King's Heath Station, while opposite are two vaguely Dutch-styled, Art Nouveau brick and stone-faced shops. Bourne's corn merchant shop occupies the end premises and next door are the offices of the Britannic Assurance Company. Further down beyond the tramcar and before the double-bay windows of the Station Hotel, a few old cottages have survived. (Commercial postcard)

The village of King's Heath, known as *Kyngesheth* in 1511, grew in a linear pattern in the nineteenth century along what later became the High Street. Standing outside the Hope chapel in the late 1950s at the railway station end of High Street is bus 2067 (JOJ 67), a Metro-Cammell-body Daimler CVD6. Turning out of Station Road is a Jaguar Mark VII saloon which, although weighing over two tons could achieve over 110mph but couldn't stop! Behind the bus, virtually the whole length of the High Street stretches up the hill towards Vicarage Road and All Saints' Church. (R.F. Mack)

At one time the shop on the corner of High Street and Station Road, which dates from the period of the First World War, was occupied by Alfred Hobday, a piano dealer but by about 1950 it is being used as a café judging by the net curtains and the stacked chairs. Parked in Station Road is a 1937 Standard Flying Nine saloon. On High Street is Hedley James, a gentlemen's tailor while outside the shops is a 1949-vintage

Austin A40 van and a Fordson 5cwt van. Although the trams had been replaced by buses some months before, the tram tracks and the associated stone sets still remain, glistening after recent rain. (Birmingham Central Reference Library)

The Parade is a typical interwar row of shops built in about 1930. This row of ten shops was set back from the rest of the older High Street. This was going to be the precursor of a widening of the A435 which was oft-suggested but never implemented. The Kingsway Picture Theatre was still a cinema in 1964 when bus 3366 (366 KOV), a Daimler Fleetline CRG6LX with a MCCW H43/33F body stood outside the newsagents shop with its weighing machine, when setting down a passenger. (R.H.G. Simpson)

At the one end of the shops was the Kingsway Cinema. This was designed by Horace Bradley and opened on 2 March 1925 with a three-year old film called *Down to the Sea in Ships*. The drama was set in the 1800s starring William Walcott as a devout Quaker who controls a fleet of whaling ships that sails from New Bedford, Massachusetts. His granddaughter was played by the future 'It Girl', Clara Bow in her first major film role. The Kingsway was converted to 'talkies' in 1931 and survived for nearly another fifty years until it closed on 3 May 1980 to become a Bingo Hall, which it still is in 2007. (Commercial postcard)

Located in High Street on the corner of York Road, the present Hare & Hounds building was opened in 1907 on the site of an earlier hostelry. Built for the Holts Brewery, the pub was built in 1906 to the designs of Samuel Owen who had designed the Kings Head at Bearwood. In March 1975 the interior still retained most of the original fixtures and fittings including being lined with Maws creamy green tiling. It also had a huge dark wood and mirrored bar-back with the Holt's Squirrel incorporated into the design. The rebuilding of the interior in 1983 rather took away some of the pub's original character. (Birmingham Central Reference)

York Road was part
of the Grange Estate
of 449 houses; this
was built in the
mid-1890s by the
Birmingham Freehold
Society for mainly
white-collar workers.
The entrance to the
Art Nouveau Hare
& Hounds public
house was in York
Road, while a few
doors away was the
Ritz Ballroom. As
with many of the side
roads off the High
Street, York Road
had clusters of retail
outlets as far as the

distant Waterloo Road and had the High Street not been such a good shopping centre, York Road would
have been self-sufficient. (Birmingham Central Reference Library)

The hourly frequency of the Midland Red service 148 to and from Evesham interspersed with rush
hour shorts on the 149 Wythall service gave Midland Red an excellent presence on Alcester Road. Bus
4023 (SHA 423), a Leyland Titan PD2/12 with a Leyland fifty-six-seat body has just left the All Saints'
Church setting-down stop beneath the trees where another Leyland is standing. Bus 4023 has exactly
fifteen minutes to get to the Station Street terminus by way of Moseley Village and the Warwickshire
CC ground in Edgbaston Road. The bus is about to pass by the entrance to Silver Street where the old
CBT steam tram depot was located, while on the left is Institute Road with the tall Gothic building of
the King's Heath Institute (built in 1878) standing against the skyline. (D.R. Harvey Collection)

King's Heath steam tram depot was in Silver Street having been opened in early 1887 for the tramway extension to King's Heath from Moseley. In the early years of BCT operation, the 1886 Beyer Peacock tram locomotive standing alongside the depot looks in really pristine condition, suggesting that it is still fairly new. It is towing one of the original 1884 Falcon trams. Trailers like this one had six side windows and seats for fifty-two passengers. Silver Street was closed as an operating depot when the CBT steam tram operation came to an end on 31 December 1906. The steam stock had to be out of the depot by the commencement of the electric trams on New Year's Day 1907, but one locomotive developed a fault, got left behind and was still there when the Corporation wired up the depot, which was then used from 1 April 1908 to 31 December 1911 operating some open-top trams in the 31-40 series. (F. Moore)

The CBT steam tram stands outside King's Heath School on the corner of Institute Road, at the King's Heath terminus. This school was built in 1878 in a typical Board School Gothic style with a large

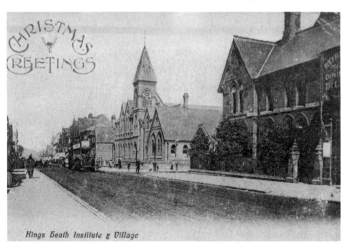

assembly hall. The landmark feature of the school was its ventilation tower which was capped with a decorative spire. The school was a gift at the original cost of £5,000 to King's Heath from the Nettlefold family and was further extended in 1882. It was closed as a school in 1933 and remained as an adult education centre for another fifty years and was demolished in the 1980s to be replaced by the Scots Corner retail outlet. (Commercial postcard)

In 1912, just before the original allocation of class 71 cars was replaced by the new 401 class trams with their air and oil brakes, car 96 is picking up passengers outside King's Heath School on the corner of Institute Road. The driver had to prepare to drive away through the piles of horse manure. On the left at 130 High Street are the premises of T. Avery who were ironmongers and still trading some twenty-five years later. The round-topped tower with the clock is the Hare & Hounds on the corner of York Road.(Commercial postcard)

Air and oil brake car 415, in its March 1947 livery waits in the middle of High Street at the terminus of the 40 route to Hill Street with its trolley pole already turned for the return to Birmingham. To the right, on the corner of Kingsfield Road, are the electrical contractors and plumbers, the Lea Brothers and next door is George Mason, the Birmingham-based family grocers whose headquarters were in Bradford Street. About to 'under-take' the tram on 9 July 1949 is a Rover Sports saloon, while travelling into the city on the 35 service is one of Yardley Wood garage's Brush-bodied Leyland Titan PD2/1s. (T.J. Edgington)

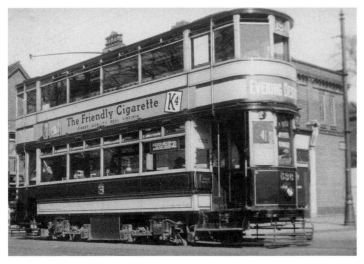

On its way out of King's Heath at Kingsfield Road on its way to Alcester Lanes End is car 536. By 9 April 1939, this UEC-bodied, sixty-two-seat, 40hp bogie car of 1913 had been re-motored with GEC WT 32/R 70hp units in 1927 and it was around this time that the balconies were enclosed. This tram had been at Hockley until the Handsworth routes were abandoned where their larger motors gave it a turn of speed which was wasted on Moseley Road. By November 1940 it had gone to Selly Oak depot's Bristol Road services where its 35mph plus top speed would be better appreciated. (J.H. Taylforth collection)

The 1920s premises on the corner of Kingsfield Road were, by August 1993, occupied by Feminine, a ladies' dress shop, something of a change since the days when it had been a plumbers' merchant! Kingsfield Road was named after Kingsfield House, a large Regency house which was the home of the brass founder, J.H. Nettlefold, who lived there until his death in 1881. Bus 3239 (H 239 LOM), one of the forty 'brake-squealing' Scania N113DR vehicles bought by West Midlands Travel to get rid of Metrobuses on the 50 route, is travelling out of Birmingham on the 50 route to Druids Heath. Behind the bus, it is noticeable that the original late Victorian buildings had been replaced in the 1960s. (D.R. Harvey)

The crossover for the trams terminating at King's Heath is just behind four-wheeled car 416. On 2 September 1949, this tram is about to return to the city on a 40 service to Hill Street via Leopold Street, for which these air and oil brake cars had been specifically modified in 1912. It is often forgotten that these fifty open-balcony 401 class trams were the backbone of all the Moseley Road tram services from their introduction until the closure of the services on 1 October 1949. Around the Vicarage Road junction, car 425 is working on the 48 service to King's Heath from High Street and a distant tram working all the way to Alcester Lanes End on the 42 route. (T.J. Edgington)

At the outer end of High Street, on the corner with Vicarage Road, is All Saints' Church, with its graceful spire dominating the skyline. The church was designed by F. Preedy and was completed in 1859; it was extended in 1883 to the designs of the well-known Birmingham architect J.A. Chatwin, but was rebuilt again with a spire tower and enlarged nave in 1899. All Saints' Church, like all good churches, can be seen from some distance away as it stands at 517ft above sea level, which is within 3ft of being the highest point in King's Heath. About ten years after its final rebuild, Corporation UEC-bodied electric tram 88, with flop-over destination boards and the destination letter M, waits at the King's Heath terminus before returning to Hill Street. (Commercial postcard)

The Alcester Road was used by Midland Red on their way out of the city to Wythall, Redditch, Alcester and Evesham. The main service was the 148 to Evesham, but the short working was to the White Swan, Wythall as service 149. A 1939 Midland Red SOS FEDD with a Brush H30/26F body, 2353 (FHA 857), is travelling along High Street, King's Heath with All Saints' Parish Church in the background. The Midland Red is opposite the subterranean public lavatories which were located in the middle of Vicarage Road. They were closed in 1993. (F.W. York/R.F. Mack)

Crossing High Street at Vicarage Road was the Outer Circle number 11 bus route which had been introduced as a complete twenty-five mile route on 7 April 1926. The bus is turning right out of Vicarage Road and will travel the short distance along Alcester Road South before turning into Addison Road. In 1958, bus 1115 (CVP 215), a 1937 Daimler COG5 with an MCCW H30/24R body is straddling the Belisha Crossing in front of All Saints' Church in 1958 as it begins the manoeuvre when surprisingly working a full duty on the Outer Circle. (F.W. York/R.F. Mack)

When the trams were abandoned, the replacement bus services were unable to just stop in the middle of King's Heath High Street and turn back to the city. A turning circle had to be found and so the original 49 route turned right in front of Flowerdew's butchers shop into Vicarage Road and as 2853 (JOJ 853) is doing in this picture, turned immediately left into All Saints Road. This bus, a 1952 Daimler CVG6 with a Crossley H30/25R body, was one of twenty of the class which were transferred to Moseley Road garage during 1965 when the 'New-Look' front CVD6s were being withdrawn. Behind the bus, on 6 October 1967, as well as the Austin Mini-Countryman, is the Edwardian block with the legend Hedges Pharmacy on the top of the Dutch-style gable on Alcester Road South. (F.W. York)

The row of shops on the left includes the aforementioned Hedges Pharmacy as open-balcony four-wheeler vehicle 412 travels into King's Heath from the Alcester Lanes End terminus. The lady passenger sitting in the motorcycle combination, next to the post box seems unaware of the tramcar approaching from the opposite direction. The tram has still got destination flop-over boards suggesting that this is before 1915 when they were replaced by number boxes mounted from the ceiling of the balcony. (Commercial postcard)

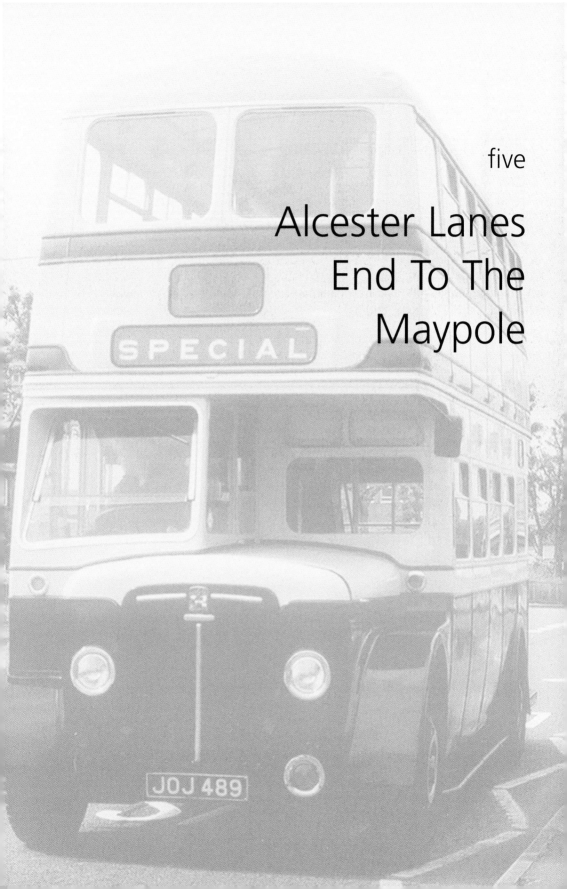

five

Alcester Lanes End To The Maypole

Travelling out of King's Heath along Alcester Road South is car 414. It is working on the 42 service in February 1949 having just passed Middleton Road. It is about to cross the junction with Howard Road. The tram is just over half a mile away from its destination. The Victorian houses behind the trees were part of a small row located around the Howard Road East junction. (F.N. Lloyd Jones)

On 6 January 1926, the newly built semi-detached houses on the corner of Howard Road make a considerable contrast with the early nineteenth-century cottages which stood between the distant Albert Road cul-de-sac and Howard Road East. The tall building beyond Albert Road is a three-storey villa dating from the end of the nineteenth century. To the right alongside the gable end of the last cottage was a footpath known as 'the Jetty' which led to Wheeler's Lane. The Alcester Road South is deserted with the empty tram lines disappearing towards King's Heath. (Birmingham Central Reference Library)

Passing the ivy-covered cottage in Alcester Road South as it approaches the junction with Howard Road East is car 445. It is working on the 42 service and will shortly begin the distant steady climb towards the Alcester Lane terminus. The tram seems well laden with passengers who would face a long walk if they had to go on to the Maypole area unless they caught an express service number 35 bus. This bus service had protected fares which were half as much again but it was much quicker than the tram! (A.K. Terry)

Having replaced the trams, the buses going only as far as King's Heath had to use side roads as a long loop in order to regain Alcester Road South but face back into the city. 2036 (JOJ 36), a Metro-Cammell-bodied Daimler CVD6, is in All Saints Road and is about to turn left into Howard Road when working on a 48A short working service in about 1959. The houses in All Saints Road were at an important location with regard to the growth of King's Heath with those at the Vicarage Road end being Victorian terraces and villas while those just behind the bus dated from the 1920s. (R.F. Mack/A.B. Cross)

Bus 1939 (HOV 939), an exposed-radiator Daimler CVD6 with an MCCW H30/24R body is travelling towards the bus stop near to Stone Road. It has just overtaken a Vauxhall Velox EIP and a man walking his dog. The Daimler CVD6 vehicles were fitted with very quiet, slightly under-powered but extremely refined 8.6 litre Daimler CD6 engines. These buses worked for about fifteen years on the Moseley Road services until replaced by the KOV-registered Daimler Fleetlines in 1964. (A.D. Broughall)

Passing the double junction of Tenbury Road and Featherstone Road is four-wheeled car 430. It is travelling towards Alcester Lanes End when working on the 42 route in August 1948. Behind the tram are some of the large Victorian houses which were built in this part of King's Heath. (Dr D. Griffiths)

As the car owner gets into his Wolseley 12/48 Series III vehicle, two trams of the 401 class stand near the Taylor Road junction waiting for their turn to move to the terminus stub and then change tracks to load up outside the Kings Arms. The Alcester Lanes End terminus was just over a furlong away and although none of the Moseley Road routes were on reserved track in this outer section of the route, the road was sufficiently wide that other traffic could pass on either side of the parked trams. Car 437, repainted on 21 February 1949 is working on the 39 service from Hill Street. By way of contrast car 419, working on the 42 service hadn't been repainted since September 1940! (A.N.H. Glover)

After the government policy of bus deregulation on 1 October 1986, the Moseley Road/Alcester Road corridor became a target for some very intensive competition between West Midlands Travel and Smiths of Shenington. In 1990, vehicle XJA 546L, a seventeen-year old ex-SELNEC PTE Park Royal-bodied Daimler 'Fleetline' CRG6LXB passes the Taylor Road junction on the 50Y route, painted with the brown, orange and white livery of Your Bus. The operator initiated a 'bus war' on the 50 service which, for a time, claimed to have the most buses working on a route anywhere in Britain. (D.R. Harvey)

Leaving the Alcester Lanes End bus stop on its way towards the Maypole and the Druids Heath Estate is bus 2350 (LOA 350X), a Mark I 73-seat MCW Metrobus. Metrobuses worked on routes 48 and 50 from about 1981 until the advent of the Scanias in 1990. Bus 2350, a West Midlands PTE bus, entered service in September 1981 and has passed a Mark II Metrobus 2687 (A687 UOE), which is about to leave the bus stop outside the Kings Arms and to travel into the city. (D.R. Harvey)

A never-ending procession of trams always seemed to be in the vicinity of the Alcester Lanes End terminus outside the Kings Arms public house. This present building replaced a much older hostelry which was a contemporary of the Alcester Turnpike toll house. This stood near the corner of Taylor Road. The old inn was therefore the Georgian equivalent of a motorway service centre as it catered for the needs of the eighteenth and nineteenth-century travelling man. The present pub dates from 1911 and was designed in a mock Tudor-style by William Jenkins for the Holder's Brewery. Car 426 stands outside the Kings Arms, known locally as 'the Knob', when working back to Moseley Road depot on 18 July 1949. These open-balcony trams ran on average some 858,000 miles in their thirty-seven years of service; one wonders if a vintage bus dating from 1970 would be welcomed today as the main type of service bus? In the foreground is a 1931-registered Austin Seven. (C.C. Thornburn)

Car 75, one of the open-platform vestibule and open-balcony UEC Radial trucked trams of 1907 stands at the Alcester Lanes End terminus before the houses from the corner of Woodthorpe Road were converted to shops around the period of the First World War. The tram is going by way of Balsall Heath on its way back to the Hill Street terminus. Beyond the terminus lay open fields and a few scattered farms and cottages and so the terminus was never extended during the lifetime of the trams. It also explains why, after the decision had been made to undertake no more tramway extensions in about 1928, the express bus service with protected fares was introduced to the Maypole. (D.R. Harvey collection)

On 10 September 1949, UEC car 301, the first of this class, stands at the terminus of route 42. This was its first day in service from Moseley Road depot, but it would be withdrawn for scrapping just three weeks later. The Bundy Clock and the red tram stop are outside the Kings Head public house which for many years was the limit of urban growth along Alcester Road South, though the shops towards Woodthorpe Road date from the end of the nineteenth century. (A.N.H. Glover)

The buses which directly replaced the trams that terminated at 'the Knob' were the 48B and the 50B services. A turning circle was built between King's Heath dog track and the first of the early post-war housing on Alcester Road South. This had been built back from the main road in preparation for a dual carriageway scheme which had yet to be been implemented. In about 1957, 2066, (JOJ 66), with the 'New-Look' front is playing host to the crew of 1964, (HOV 964), which is standing next to the Bundy Clock. (D.R. Harvey collection)

There were several dog tracks in Birmingham including those at Perry Barr and Hall Green. This one was opened at the end of the 1920s, just to the north of the then municipal golf course. It was finally closed in March 1971 and the site today is the small Wynfield Gardens housing development. One of the most popular dog tracks was at Alcester Lanes End, King's Heath, which in 1929 actually held two 'speedway' or grass motorcycling meetings. The entrance is to the bottom left and visible is the greyhound racing track, the two large stands and the judge's control tower. (Birmingham Central Reference Library)

The Cocks Moor municipal golf course was opened on the last remaining piece of the 'king's heath' in 1926 with originally just fourteen holes. This part of King's Heath was an area of woodland and open grass which, although converted into the course, did manage to retain a certain historical feel. The original clubhouse was unusually built with a thatched roof on the ninety-nine-acre golf club site. It became an eighteen-hole golf course in 1936. The whole site is now part of the Cocks Moor Leisure complex. (Birmingham Central Reference Library)

Beyond the Kings Arms public house and pre-First World War housing at Alcester Lanes End, as the name suggests, the area was largely rural. On leaving 'the Knob', Alcester Road South drops gently down into the Chinn Brook Valley, which is a tributary of the River Cole. On the northern terrace of the valley was Broad Lane along which there were a number of late eighteenth-century cottages. Even in 1935, over the fields on the skyline the three-storey Victorian houses on Alcester Road South opposite Millpool Farm stood out. Beyond the Ford Y 8hp saloon car, the road rises, passing over the Stratford-upon-Avon Canal and past another row of cottages and the Horse Shoe Inn. The valley remained a rural idyll until well into the post-war era. (Birmingham Central Reference Library)

Looking northwards back across the Chinn Brook Valley on 13 July 1939, the bridge over the Stratford-upon-Avon Canal had recently been widened to accommodate the increasing traffic on the A435. This canal, branching off the slightly older Worcester Canal at Kings Norton Junction, was first proposed in 1793 but took until 1816 to complete. The Horse Shoe Inn dates from between these two dates and was a popular canal-side Mitchell & Butler's pub from the early years of the twentieth century. On the right is the Corporation bus stop for the 35 cross-city Maypole bus route, while on the left, the tobacconist's shop was also an agent for Midland Red buses and parcels. (Birmingham Central Reference Library)

Metro-Cammell-bodied Daimler CVD6s, 1937 (HOV 937), is on an inbound 48 route via Balsall Heath in about 1958. It is passing the old farm outbuildings and barns from the Mill Pool Hill Farm. This was an obstacle to traffic on Alcester Road South for many years, remaining until the late 1990s before demolition took place thereby enabling the road to become a dual carriageway. In the distance, a Ford 5cwt van is turning into Meadfoot Avenue while beyond it is still open agricultural land. (R.F. Mack)

By the summer of 1993, when the MCW Metrobus Mark I was still a common bus on the Alcester Road services, 2356 (LOA 356X), a 1981-built DR 102/22 model owned by this time by West Midlands Travel stands in the shadow of the 1960s-built multi-storey blocks of Hillcroft and Heath Houses. The closure of Moseley Road garage in 1972 meant that all bus operation on the Moseley Road and Balsall Heath services was transferred to Liverpool Street garage in Bordesley. In the early 1990s only the last few hundred yards of Alcester Road South from the city boundary had been widened into a dual carriageway. (D.R. Harvey)

Leaving the nearest bus stop to the by now demolished Maypole public house is 4387, (BV52 OBE). This Dennis Trident 334BR with an Alexander H47/28F body entered service in December 2002. It is about to continue to the Druids Heath terminus on 5 June 2005. To the left of the bus is the mixed height development just off Alcester Road South while behind the bus shelters is the late 1960s Maypole shopping precinct which was already in its death throes as its demolition would be completed in early 2007. (D.R. Harvey)

Redolent of an earlier age of public transport, the author's bus, former Birmingham City Transport 2489 (JOJ 489), a 1950 Crossley DD42/6, pulls away from the Alcester Road South bus stop on 5 June 2005. Although Crossleys were not regularly employed on services along Moseley Road, occasionally they would come off an Outer Circle duty and run into the city centre as a service extra. (D.R. Harvey)

On Thursday 16 March 1934, 509 (OC 509), a six-month old Birmingham-built Metro-Cammell-bodied Morris-Commercial Imperial, a chassis of which only eighty-three were built, stands at the almost rural terminus at the City of Birmingham boundary where Alcester Road South met Druids Lane. Just in front of the bus is a substantial wooden passenger shelter of the sort usually more associated with tram termini. Gradually suburbia was creeping out from Alcester Lanes End and soon would engulf the land up to the Solihull boundary on the north side of Maypole Lane. The bus is working on the cross-city, semi-express number 17 service to Chester Road, Erdington. (Birmingham Central Reference Library)

THE MAYPOLE HOTEL & TERMINUS . KINGS HEATH

The opening up of the land beyond Alcester Lanes End in the 1920s and the reluctance of the Corporation to extend the tram route to the city boundary at the Maypole resulted in the introduction of the cross-city route 17 to Erdington on 19 March 1928 which in turn became the 35 route southbound and the 17 northbound on 17 August 1936. The large Maypole public house, as a sign of encroaching civilisation, had been opened on 17 July 1936 and was closed in 2002 to be replaced by a hotel complex. The nearest of the two virtually new Metro-Cammell-bodied Daimler COG5s (which had both entered service on 1 June 1935) has its destination blind set to Erdington 17 and is bus 710 (AOP 710) while the second bus, 708 (AOP 708), shows a route blind for the 35 southbound service. (Commercial postcard courtesy of A. Maxam)

The express bus service was cut back to work only as far as the city centre on 11 September 1939 as a wartime economy measure. In June 1949, the almost new 1667 (HOV 667), a Leyland Titan PD2/1 with

a brush H30/24R body, which had entered service in October 1948, waits outside the Maypole to return to Station Street on the 35 service in company with 165 (EOG 165), a 1938-vintage Daimler COG5 with an MCCW body. When the Moseley Road tram routes were abandoned on 1 October 1949, so the 35 bus service was replaced by the 48 bus service. (G.F. Douglas, courtesy of A.D. Packer)

Standing in the turning circle outside the Maypole public house in about 1955 are two representatives of the buses which almost exclusively ran the Balsall Heath, Moseley and King's Heath bus services for about fourteen years. Metro-Cammell-bodied 'New-Look' front Daimler CVD6, 2055 (JOJ 55) is waiting to return to Albert Street on the 50 service while behind is bus 1949 (HOV 949), an exposed-radiator CVD6 (just one year older than the other vehicle) working on the 48 service back to Paradise Street by way of Balsall Heath. (A.B. Cross)

Since the demise of the Your Bus operation a number of other independent bus companies have tried their luck on the Maypole services along sections of the A435. Although none of the buses are working on service 50, Choice Travel, operating from Wednesfield was using the vehicle Y386 HKE, a Dennis Dart SLF with a Plaxton 'Mini-Pointer' body on their 634 service. This links the Maypole junction where the pub had been recently replaced by a hotel complex at the end of 2006, with Northfield. It has just overtaken 4152 (Y747 TOH), a Dennis Trident with an Alexander H47/28F body dating from May 2001 which is about to turn into Maypole Lane as it works on the 69 route to Solihull. The third bus is another one of Choice Travel's Dennis Darts waiting to take on its next duty. (D.R. Harvey)

The orange and white-liveried Your Bus fleet, originally owned by Smiths of Shenington, was taken over as a 'low-cost' operator by West Midlands Travel after a few years of offering a real threat to the latter's operations, especially on the service to the Maypole. Still using the 50Y route number, an Optare DP49F-bodied DAF SB220, 6 (F372 KBW), dating from February 1990, is in Bells Lane on the Druids Heath Estate having just left the terminus on 5 February 1997. (D.R. Harvey)

The Druids Heath Terminus

The Druids Heath council estate belonged to an area which became part of Birmingham in 1911 and was still largely farmland until the end of the 1950s. By the mid-1960s the housing estate was set out and was still largely a building site when the 48 bus service was extended from the Maypole via Druids Lane and Bells Lane to a new terminus at the junction of Druids Lane on 10 July 1966. On 22 February 1999, 4004 (S404 NVP), an Optare-bodied DAF DB250LF, one of a production batch of twenty which were the first of a new generation of low floor buses, turns into the terminus loop at the Bells Lane–Druids Lane junction with the early 1970s terraced houses in the background. (D.R. Harvey)

Waiting to return to the city centre at the Druids Heath terminus on 16 June 2000 is V929 FWS. This is a Dennis Trident 2 with an Alexander ALX400 seventy-four seat body and was being demonstrated to Travel West Midlands with some success as large orders soon followed. The Alexander body was ordered and subsequently fitted to both Dennis Trident and Volvo B7TL chassis. (A. Hayward)

Opposite above: On a leafless winter's day in 1973, a West Midlands Daimler Fleetline CRG6LX 4323 (NOB 323M), with a standard PTE-specification Park Royal body, waits at the Bundy Clock before heading back to the city on the 48 route. The bus is still fitted with its chrome nut-guard rings suggesting that the bus is almost new. (D.R. Harvey collection)

Opposite below: About the time when Billy Graham came to preach for seven days at the end of June and the beginning of July 1984 at Villa Park, bus 2749 (A749 WVP), carries advertisements for this event. The bus (an MCW Metrobus II DR102/27 with an MCW H43/30F body) is leaving the Druids Heath terminus on the 50 route on 21 June 1984. (D.R. Harvey collection)

BIRMINGHAM CORPORATION
TRAMWAY & OMNIBUS DEPT.

Transport Facilities 1935

COUNCIL HOUSE,
BIRMINGHAM.

A. C. BAKER
GENERAL MANAGER.

Birmingham Corporation Tramway and Omnibus Department's 'Transport Facilities' booklet was upgraded every year and was in fact a fold-up bus, tram and trolley-bus timetable. The ink drawings were altered every few years, though in 1937 the municipal undertaking's name was itself changed to Birmingham City Transport.

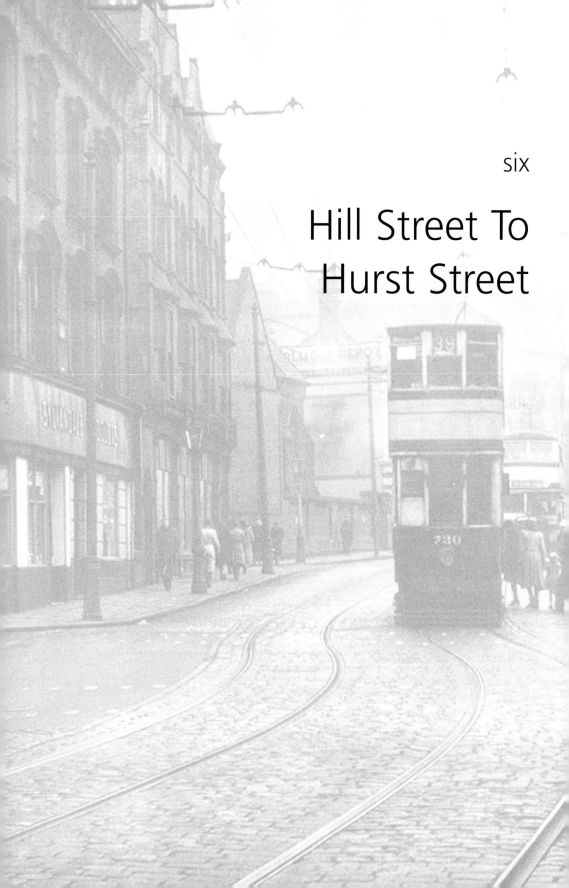

six

Hill Street To
Hurst Street

On 27 July 1940, one of the 70hp totally enclosed bogie tram cars of 1913, 522 stands in
Navigation Street when loading up with passengers going on to Cannon Hill on the 37 service.
This tram was rebuilt in late 1928 with enclosed balconies and a top deck fitted with eight
windows. It is being overtaken by a 1935 Morris Ten-Six car which is dwarfed by the seven-storey
Queen's Hotel. Behind the tram on 27 July 1940 is the as yet undamaged steel and canopy roof
designed by E.A. Cowper over New Street Station. It was 212ft wide and contained some 1,050
tons of wrought and cast iron as well as 115 tons of glass. The structure was badly damaged by
bombs on Tuesday 19 November 1940 and again on Thursday 10 April 1941. (F.W. Goudie)

The 17 July 1949 was an uncharacteristically wet day as car 424, one of the UEC-bodied,
Spencer-Dawson air and oil brake cars fitted rigidly with Mountain and Gibson 7ft 6in. trucks
leaves its Navigation Street terminus. The tram is working on the 41 route to Trafalgar Road by
way of Leopold Street and is turning into Hill Street. In front of the tram is Queen's Drive. This
private right of way separated the old LNWR side of New Street Station from the later Midland
Railway side while linking the Hill Street entrance to Worcester Street. (C.C. Thornburn)

Not quite what it seems! Due to track repairs in Digbeth, on Bonfire Night 1939, all the Moseley Road tram routes were diverted to the corresponding Alcester Lanes End via Balsall Heath 39 service in Hill Street. The UEC, sixty-two-seater tram 512 mounted on M and G Burnley maximum traction bogies had been delivered in October 1913 with open balconies but these were enclosed in the late 1920s and later it was re-motored with GEC WT32R 70hp motors in 1927. Car 512 arrived at Moseley Road depot on 2 April 1939 and had been fitted with an old set of destination blinds which showed the city terminus as the short-lived 1920s Dale End location. (A.N.H. Glover)

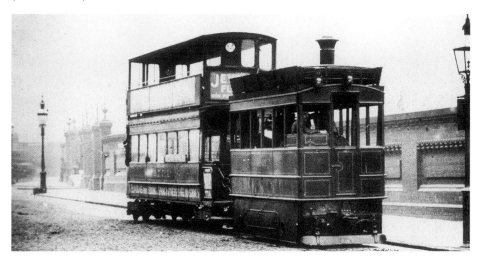

Waiting at the Hill Street terminus, with the decorative entrance pillars to Queen's Drive in the distance, is an 1885 Falcon steam tram locomotive. Built to Falcon design, this trailer is double ended and has seven side windows. The tram is working on the M service to Moseley Village. Unlike the subsequent Corporation electric tramcars, the CBT steam trams ran around Hill Street, Station Street and John Bright Street in a loop so that the tram locomotive did not have to run round the trailer. The tram is standing alongside the parapet walls of New Street Station. It is loading up next to the pavement after the introduction of kerb-side loading in 1905, just one year before the conversion to electric operation. (D.R. Harvey collection)

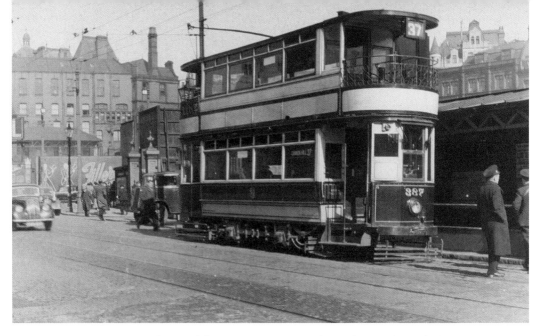

Car 387 was sent to Moseley Road depot in January 1945 and was subsequently overhauled at Kyotts Lake Works in the following March. It remained as one of seven cars of the 301 class at Moseley Road and surprisingly ran at Washwood Heath depot for another two years. The tram is waiting at the Hill Street shelters in about 1946 and is roughly in the same spot as the steam tram some forty years before. It is working on the 37 service to Cannon Hill. Coming out of Queen's Drive is a pre-war Fordson 7V lorry, while about to overtake the parked tram is a Morris 8 Series E. (Burrows Brothers)

Sunday 2 October 1949 was the first day of bus operation on the 48 service to the Maypole. A sparkling 1953 (HOV 953), Daimler CVD6 with a Metro-Cammell H30/24R body, is loading up passengers in roughly the same place in Hill Street as the CBT steam tram and the Corporation tram 387 in the previous views. The bus stop railings behind the bus are however not those of the terminus which was initially in Paradise Street between Hill Street and Suffolk Street, opposite the Birmingham and Midland Institute. (S.N.J. White)

It is 1951 in Paradise Street as 1949-vintage Daimler CVD6 bus, 1933 (HOV 933), working on the 49 service to King's Heath via Leopold Street, jostles for position at its terminus stop with a departing Midland Red wartime bus. 1933 would eventually turn left at the row of shops leading into Suffolk Street. On the left, parked outside the showrooms of Patrick Motors is Midland Red 2440 (GHA 794), an 'unfrozen' Leyland Titan TD7 with a Northern Counties body working on the long 125 route to Dudley and Wolverhampton. The car traffic includes a brand-new 1951 Riley RMA 1.5 litre, a pre-war Ford Y 8hp Tudor, an Austin A40 Dorset and two 1948 Hillman Minx Phase II vehicles. (Birmingham Central Reference Library)

The gas showrooms in Paradise Street overlooked the junction with Suffolk Street. In early 1962, Daimler CVD6, 1959 (HOV 959), has already unloaded the last of its inbound passengers in Paradise Street. The bus is turning the corner into Suffolk Street prior to loading up again at a new terminus which was introduced on 1 December 1961 for both the 48 and 49 services. Bus 1959 is working on the 49B service to Moseley Village via Leopold Street. (R.F. Mack)

In 1965, with the West End Cinema still open and the shops and offices in Easy Row still standing, bus 2049, (JOJ 49), an MCCW-bodied 'New-Look' front Daimler CVD6 which entered service in December 1950, is beginning to pull away from the lay-by in Suffolk Street when working on the 49F short working service to Moseley Village. By this date 2049 has lost its municipal crest on the front cowling, has had its front wings cut back to allow better airflow around the brakes and received the black waistrail fleet numbers. (A.B. Cross)

Turning out of Navigation Street and about to cross in front of the junction with John Bright Street and into Hill Street is bus 1935, (HOV 935). This Daimler CVD6 is working on the out of city service 48 to the Maypole in about 1961. Unusually this bus was sold to Wolverhampton Corporation in October 1964 and survived until February 1967. (R.H.G. Simpson)

Although the tram tracks remain, they had been abandoned by the Moseley Road services which started in Hill Street over one year earlier. They were used in order for the trams on the Bristol Road and Cotteridge services to gain access to the tram works at Kyotts Lake Road in Sparkbrook. A former 1950 Commercial Motor Show exhibit, 2033, (JOJ 33), with its extra piece of chrome trim on the top of the radiator cowling, travels into the city on a 48A service. In the distance is the tower of the Birmingham Hippodrome while behind the Ansells-owned Grapes public house is the huge bulk of the Futurist cinema which had opened in July 1919 and on 18 March 1929 became the first cinema in Birmingham to show a 'talkie', with Al Jolson in *The Singing Fool*. (D.A. Jones)

With the still relatively new Midland Railway side of New Street Station in the background, two of Birmingham & District Omnibus' horse buses pass each other in Hill Street, on a service which had been taken over from Messrs Twist and Young in September 1895. The horse bus on the left is unloading passengers on its way to the city terminus in New Street while the one on the right is leaving to follow the CBT Moseley steam tram route as far as the Coach and Horses pub on the corner of Mary Street and Edward Road. (D.R. Harvey Collection)

The withdrawal of Moseley Road's allocation of 'New-Look' front Daimler CVD6s, 2031-2070, took place between November 1965 and February 1966. To partially overcome shortages, the garage received sixteen of the 1952-built Daimler CVG6s with Crossley H30/25R bodies from the nearby Yardley Wood garage. Travelling down Station Street from its junction with John Bright Street on 11 July 1968 is car 2856, (JOJ 856), on the 48 route to 'Druids Heath Estate', a display later reduced to just 'Druids Heath'. This way out of the city was introduced on St Valentine's Day 1965. (F.W. York)

Loading up with passengers in the middle of Hill Street at the traffic light-controlled junction with Smallbrook Street is 1925 vintage car 730. These totally enclosed-bodied, 16-ton tramcars of the 702 class were equipped with GEC 40hp motors and regarded as somewhat slow. This did not matter too much on most of Moseley Road depot's routes but they were only just adequate when fully loaded and working on the 1 in 13 hill in Leopold Street. The tramcar is shown here working on an outbound 39 service to Alcester Lanes End and being shadowed by a 1938 Daimler COG5. On the left in the distance is the car showroom of Colmore Depot in Station Street, St Jude's Church and on the corner of Smallbrook Street is Smarts who were household furnishers. (F.N. Lloyd Jones)

Standing on the cobbles in Dudley Street is 2067, (JOJ 67), a Daimler CVD6 with a Metro-Cammell H30/24R body which had entered service on New Year's Day 1951. In the background are the remnants of New Street Station's once-impressive roof. Looking very smart, bus 2067 is working on the 48 service to the Maypole via Balsall Heath in about 1958. The advertisement on the bus is for Fillerys Toffees, made in Greet in Birmingham. (D.R. Harvey collection)

2034, (JOJ 34), heels over as it takes the turn from Dudley Street into Pershore Street when working on the 48B route to Alcester Lanes End in about 1958. On the right is the four-storey Sydenham Hotel which in earlier days had been the main commercial hotel for Birmingham's market area. Behind the bus is Worcester Street which led to New Street, with Brooke's opticians on the Dudley Street corner and the Le Brasseur surgical supplies shop on the right. (D.R. Harvey collection)

Travelling into the city along Pershore Street and about to turn into Dudley Street and pass beneath Smallbrook Queensway and the Ringway Centre buildings is an early standard West Midlands PTE double-decker. Bus 4327, (NOB 327M), a Daimler Fleetline CRG6LX with a Park Royal H43/33F body had entered service in September 1973. It is working on the 49 route from King's Heath in about 1974. Today, Pershore Street is part of Birmingham's thriving 'China Town' area, though even in 1974 there were a number of excellent Cantonese restaurants. (A.J. Douglas)

After deregulation in October 1986, a new challenge to West Midlands Travel began when Smiths of Shenington set up in competition to operate buses along the lucrative Moseley Road-Alcester Road corridor. Their Your Bus services were initially operated by a variety of second-hand double-deckers, which although not exactly immaculate, were 'cheap and cheerful' and despite their age provided high frequency headways on their 50Y service. The YNA 351M (formerly the 7396 of Greater Manchester PTE), a Daimler Fleetline CRG6LX with a Northern Counties body, loads up in Edgbaston Street in about 1988 between the distant elevated Smallbrook Queensway and the Rag Market near to St Martin's Parish Church. (D.R. Harvey)

The 35 route terminated in Station Street and having gone through the market area the route turning left out of Pershore Street into Bromsgrove Street in front of Samuel Kershaw's war surplus and radio shop. Bus 1677, (HOV 677), a 1948 Leyland Titan PD2/1 with a Brush body is working on the 35 service on 25 September 1949, less than a week before it was replaced by the 48 route when the King's Heath trams were abandoned. (G.F. Douglas courtesy of A.D. Packer)

The Ringway Centre (as the five-storey building on the south side of Smallbrook Ringway was known), leapt over Hurst Street on two pairs of raked columns, while in the subterranean depths was the first pedestrian subway in Britain which had been opened in April 1959. The completed sweep of the buildings was accomplished in 1961 while the first section of the road had been opened by Earnest Marples on 11 March 1960. In 1965, 3375, (375 KOV), a Daimler Fleetline CRG6LX with a Metro-Cammell body passes the entrance to the new Albany Hotel as it travels into the city on route 48K. (R.H.G. Simpson)

On a dull day in 1938, totally enclosed Brush-bodied bogie car 731 trundles down Hill Street and approaches the junction with Smallbrook Street when working on the short 37 service to Cannon Hill. Coming into Hill Street from Hurst Street is another member of the 702-731 class. On its right is the Empire Palace Theatre which had opened in 1894, eventually becoming part of the Moss Empires circuit. It failed to survive an air raid in the spring of 1941 but was only demolished in about 1951. Towering over the trams is George Hull's four-storey dry-salter, oil, varnish and paint manufacturer's premises. (S.L. Smith)

In the distance in Hurst Street is the long-since demolished tower of the Birmingham Hippodrome. The theatre opened on 9 October 1892 as the 'Tower of Varieties and Circus' and survives today as the home of the Birmingham Royal Ballet and Birmingham's premier Christmas pantomime. Bus 1966, (HOV 966), a Daimler CVD6 with a Metro-Cammell H30/24R body which entered service in late 1949, has travelled down Hurst Street and is about to cross Bromsgrove Street when working on the 48B route to Alcester Lanes End in the late 1950s. (W.J. Haynes)

seven

Balsall Heath And The Chinese Railway – A Circular Journey

Once south of Bromsgrove Street, the trams and buses passed into an area of factories such as C.W. Hayles who were nail manufacturers based at 164, Hurst Street near to the Sherlock Street junction. In about 1960, 2049, (JOJ 49), takes a fairly light load of passengers on the 49B service to Moseley Village along Hurst Street before travelling through the edge of Balsall Heath to Leopold Street. Parked on Hayle's forecourt are a Standard 10, an early Morris Minor 1000 and a 1958 Ford Consul II 204E. (R.H.G. Simpson)

Towering over the junction of Sherlock Street and Hurst Street was the four-storey building occupied by the post office. A quite rare six-cylinder Austin Hereford A70 follows the 1958 bus, (HOV 958), out of Hurst Street in about 1957. The bus is about to turn right into Sherlock Street and follow the Commer van as far as Gooch Street. The Daimler CVD6 bus is working on the 48 service to the Maypole. (R.F. Mack)

The depressing, half-destroyed inner areas of Balsall Heath were littered with what local children called 'bomb-building' sites, rows of back-to-back courtyards and miserable Victorian terraces and buildings propped up with temporary wooden buttresses. The totally enclosed Brush bogie car 722 travels through such a landscape in Sherlock Street as it makes its way out of the city on the 37 route to Cannon Hill. The tram will continue along Sherlock Street before turning left into St Luke's Road which was taken by both the 37 and 39 tram services. It is about to cross the junction with Gooch Street where the same inbound tram routes on the 'Chinese Railway' come back into the city. (C.W. Routh)

Having travelled along Sherlock Street to within one block of the Pershore Road junction, the 37 and 39 tram routes turned left into St Luke's Road which was, in 1949, still part of the Inner Circle 8 bus route. Parked on the left is a 1934 Morris Oxford Six. The Gouch family initially sold off land for better quality houses in the Sherlock Street area Balsall Heath. Open-balcony car 402 and has just turned into St Luke's Road, with Edward Cogswell's greengrocery on the left and the grocery shop of Maurice Stanford on the opposite Pershore Road corner. (D.R. Harvey collection)

Car 425 (the first of the UEC four-wheeled trams to be repainted into the post-war livery on 26 September 1946) unloads and picks up passengers in St Luke's Road at the junction with Belgrave Road during 1949. The tram is working on the 39 service from Hill Street to Alcester Lanes End via Balsall Heath. The houses in this part of Balsall Heath were built in the 1870s. The tram is about to cross Belgrave Road and travel into Alexandra Road before turning left into Balsall Heath Road. (F.N. Lloyd Jones)

Once across Belgrave Road, the 37 and 39 tram routes travelled along Alexandra Road which was laid out in the 1860s and subsequently named after the Danish Princess Alexandra who had married the future Edward VII in 1863. Alexandra Road was lined with the better-quality terraced housing with decorative brickwork, bay windows and even small front gardens. The whole area had been earmarked for redevelopment since 1942, but planning blight quickened the decline of this area in the post-war years into an area notorious for prostitution. A red light in the window here was definitely not a sign of political allegiance! In about 1949, enclosed bogie car 722 is travelling outbound on a 39 service in Alexandra Road and will turn left into Balsall Heath Road. (F.N. Lloyd Jones)

The Luxor Cinema, opened in November 1913, was showing the film, *East Side of Heaven*, made in 1939 and starring Bing Crosby and Joan Blondell, when UEC-bodied four-wheeled car 418 was discharging passengers in Balsall Heath Road in 1949. The tram is working on the 37 route to Cannon Hill. Car 418 will turn hard right in front of the café and turn into Clevedon Road. This was in the heart of the intertwining tracks of Balsall Heath's 'Chinese Railway'. Trams trundled up one road and turned into another within sight of each other but never actually crossed. Just visible is another 401 class car which is travelling into the city, from right to left, along Longmore Street. (R.T. Wilson)

Coming out from the city, bogie car 726 stands outside the Luxor Cinema when working on the 37 service. It is about to get to the Longmore Street-Cox Street West junction. On the left is Foster's wine and spirit merchants while on the right in Longmore Street is Alfred Pinnick's 'complete' household furnishers. The tram has just passed over the River Rea Bridge and once it has pulled away from the Luxor Cinema, the tram will turn hard right into Clevedon Road. (C.W. Routh)

Even after about fifteen years since the abandonment of the Balsall Heath tram services in 1949, much of the area around Longmore Street had remained largely unaltered. Tarmac still covered the tram tracks and the rest of the road retained its cobbles. 2054, (JOJ 54), a Daimler CVD6 with a Metro-Cammell body crosses Balsall Heath Road on its way towards King's Heath on a 48J service. Pinnick's is still selling furniture on the corner of Balsall Heath Road while behind the bus in Longmore Street, the impressive late Victorian retail block includes a grocery business and Scrivens the opticians. On the extreme right the bus is passing the Wallace Inn with its black and white glazed tile front. (F.W.York)

Having turned out of Balsall Heath Road, the trams followed Cleveland Road with its three-storey terraced housing on the eastern side which dated from the early 1860s. Car 717 is on its way to Cannon Hill having recently been repainted in the 1946 livery but with the small, later style of fleet number. The tram has just passed a parked Standard Eight which is facing Pinnick's shop and the Luxor Cinema. (S.N.J.White)

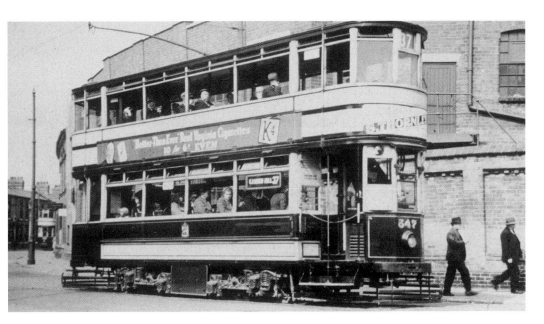

UEC-built tram 547 comes out of Clevedon Road before turning into Court Road in the foreground. Car 547 entered service in 1913 and originally had open-balconies. It was re-motored with 63hp motors in July 1927 when the tram was totally enclosed. The tram is working on the 37 service to Cannon Hill in 1939. To the right of the tram is Jakemans Walk and occupying the large factory behind car 547 is Parker & Osborne, who were glass merchants who also specialised in bathroom fittings. Their Calthorpe Works factory was destroyed in an air raid in 1941. (L.W. Perkins)

Once the trams had reached the end of Court Road on their way out of the city, the 39 service turned left into Edward Road in front of the Ansells Brewery-owned Cannon Hill public house with its mock Elizabethan gables. Today, this building is an annex for South Birmingham College. On 15 May 1947, four-wheeled car 419 (fitted with air and oil brakes), working on the 39 service, swings around in front of the pub and turns into Edward Road. On the connecting track, on the rarely-used triangle, car 389 is parked, facing Cannon Hill Road and the loop around Edgbaston and Willows Road. (D.R. Harvey collection)

A rather grubby-looking car 717 is working on the 39 service to Alcester Lanes End in 1949. The tram is about to travel over the tracks leading out of Hallam Street on the left and Lincoln Street on the right as it travels up the Edward Road hill from the distant Cannon Hill public house. On the corner is R.J. Shropshall's builder's yard which had been the site of a wartime bomb, leaving the gaping fireplace on the gable end. (F.N. Lloyd Jones)

Having passed the parked cars for sale on the Lincoln Street Motors forecourt, this Daimler Fleetline CRG6LX 3372 (372 KOV) travels through the dismal dereliction of the still partly cobbled Lincoln Street in about 1965. The bus itself has an identity problem as it is going to Moseley Village on the short working 48F, but still displays the 'TO CITY' destination. On the left is a parked Austin A35 van. (L. Mason)

Standing at the Lincoln Street–Edward Road junction on the 48 bus route is the 1107 (CVP 207), a 1937 Daimler COG5 with a 1939 MCCW H30/24R body. Alongside the bus is the Woodman public house while on the opposite side of Lincoln Street is Shropshall's builder's yard. The bus has driven up Lincoln Street in 1959 from the junction of the distant Cox Street and Cox Street West. 1107 was bought with great foresight by Barry Ware in 1964 and is still in excellent fettle. (R.F. Mack)

An Austin Cambridge 10/4 is overtaking car 301, one of the ten 301 class trams drafted into Moseley Road depot just before the route closures as trams pencilled-in for imminent scrapping. 301 is about to turn into Mary Street which will be the first time that the inbound cars on the 39 service and the outbound trams will have met since they separated in Sherlock Street. On the corner of Mary Street are the premises of Balsall Heath Motors with the red plate, 'all cars stop here', outside it. (R.T. Wilson)

Once the trams had turned right into Mary Street on their way out of Birmingham, they began the steady climb up to the junction with Park Road. The landscape of Mary Street changed into better-quality properties such as the late Victorian housing on the left. Totally enclosed Brush-bodied bogie car 719 slowly works its way up to the Park Road junction in early 1949 when working on the 39 service to Alcester Lanes End, having passed a 1948 Standard 8 convertible going towards Edward Road. (F.N. Lloyd Jones)

The open-balcony car 446 stands on the steepest section of Mary Street between Strensham Road and Edgbaston Road on 23 August 1949 and is waiting to use the crossover in order to return to Hill Street. Just behind the tram, there are seven very distinct houses which had balconies with wrought-iron balustrades and trellis work. The tram is standing at the terminus of the short working the 49 route. This air and oil brake car was last overhauled on 26 November 1947, but in September 1948 its interior was repainted. (G.F. Douglas)

Travelling into the city and picking up passengers just inside Mary Street having crossed Edgbaston Road, is totally enclosed bogie car 717. It will take the distant curve and the crossover at the terminus of route 49 before travelling down Mary Street towards Balsall Heath. On the right is the row of shops contained in the terrace of three-storey mid-nineteenth century premises. These shops included a butcher, a confectioner, a newsagent, a bookie's shop, a grocer and a gentlemen's outfitter. (J.H. Taylforth collection)

Having crossed the Edgbaston Road junction, the Corporation trams continued to follow the former CBT steam tram service on the steady climb up Park Road towards the Alcester Road junction. Air and oil brake car 406, is working on the 39 service and has caught up with the earlier UEC car 328, also on the 39 service. Car 328 had been sent to Moseley Road depot eleven months prior to the abandonment of the trams and was, like 406, broken up at Moseley Road depot. (W.A. Camwell/ Birmingham Central Reference Library)

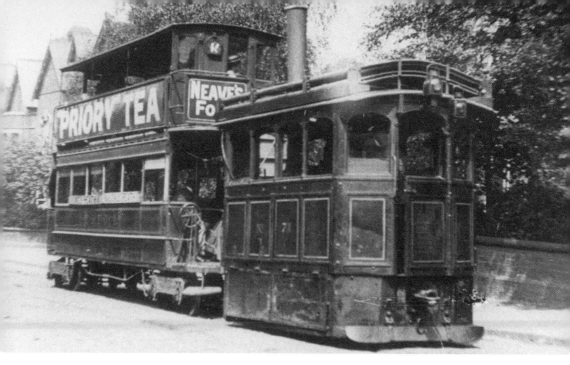

The Birmingham Central Tramways Company began operation of its steam trams to Moseley via Balsall Heath on 26 July 1886. BCT stream tram locomotive, 73, one of the Kitson locomotives of 1894, pulls an 1884 Falcon double-ended six-windowed trailer (one of the only models to have knife-board seating on the open-sided upper saloon). The tram, whose locomotive is running firebox-first, is standing in Park Road and working on the K route to King's Heath by way of Balsall Heath. (D.R. Harvey collection)

Bus 2038, (JOJ 38), had entered service on 1 November 1950 and in the following February, is still in its original condition with trafficators and wheel discs, the snow and lying slush have played havoc with the normal pristine appearance of this Birmingham bus. This Metro-Cammell-bodied Daimler CVD6 bus is in Willows Road and approaching the junction with Edgbaston Road when working out from Balsall Heath on the 48B service. (D.R. Harvey collection)

When buses replaced the tram service, the Balsall Heath services were simplified and the Park Road and Mary Street sections were suddenly without public transport for the first time in about sixty years. The buses used the former inbound tram route 37 along Lincoln Street, Hallam Street and Willows Road in both directions before turning into Edgbaston Road opposite the north-east corner of Cannon Hill Park before continuing into Salisbury Road where the Daimler COG5 946, (COH 946), stands. This 1937-built bus is working on the 48B service to Alcester Lanes End in about 1951. Bus 946 will proceed up Salisbury Road towards the junction with Alcester Road in the centre of Moseley Village, passing the turn of the century Arts and Crafts villas which still grace this part of Moseley. (S.N.J. White)

Car 440 has descended Mary Street from Alcester Road on its way into the city on the 39 service. It is 1949 and is about to leave the compulsory stop and cross Edward Road. Car 366 is travelling outbound towards Moseley. On the right is the Regency Dry Cleaners. (R.T. Wilson)

Back at Edward Road, open-balcony four-wheeled car 432 continues into Mary Street as it travels into the city during the last few months of tramcar operation in 1949, when working on the 39 route. Standing outside Frederick Pearson's newsagents, tobacconists and hairdressers shop is a mother, well-laden with her shopping and her two young daughters. Behind them and next to the post box is Mary Street's post office. (L.M. Pargetter Collection)

The 48 route used Lincoln Street on its way into the city from the Maypole and King's Heath. The bus and the man with the wheelbarrow are both passing the Erdington Laundry pick-up shop, which was one of twenty outlets in Birmingham. The roads between Balsall Heath Road and Edward Road had houses which were mainly built in the 1870s as two-up two-downs; these were something of an improvement on the back-to-back houses nearer to the city. Bus 2067, (JOJ 67), a Metro-Cammell-bodied Daimler CVD6 with a 'New-Look' front spent the whole of its fifteen-year service life working from Moseley Road. In all this time, Lincoln Street had never been resurfaced. (F.W. York/R.F. Mack)

On the 10 July 1949, the LRTL hired trams 830 and 367 to tour those routes which were due for imminent abandonment, including the Witton and Perry Barr routes and those operated by Moseley Road depot. Car 830, a Maley & Taunton air-brake bogie car with 63hp motors bodied by Short Brothers, entered service in the spring of 1929 and was chosen for the tour as it had just come out of Kyotts Lake Road Works after an overhaul. It was the only time one of these 812-class bogie cars ran on the Moseley Road services. It is travelling into the city along Cox Street West near Balsall Heath Road and is seen from the balcony of the 367. (F.N. Lloyd Jones)

During 1961, just prior to the wholesale demolition of this part of Balsall Heath, bus 2044, (JOJ 44), a Metro-Cammell-bodied Daimler CVD6, travels along Cox Street West. On the extreme right is Upper Cox Street with the round-fronted, three-storey off-licence owned by Mrs Florrie Shaylor. The bus is working on the 48 route towards Moseley where it met the 'main line' Moseley Road 50 service. (R.F. Mack)

Travelling into the city along Longmore Street and approaching Belgrave Road is 2858, (JOJ 858), a Daimler CVG6 with a Crossley H30/25R body which is working on the 48 route on 5 September 1968. The distant mid-Victorian houses are derelict while the area through which the bus is travelling has already been cleared as part of the Highgate redevelopment scheme which was begun in the 1960s. The bus is passing the Percy Shurmer School, named after Percy Shurmer (1890-1958), who took his seat at Westminster in 1945 as the local Labour MP for Sparkbrook. (F.W. York)

In 1958, when forty-one pre-war Daimler COG5 buses were brought back into service, their paintwork positively glistened as it does on 1060, (CVP 160), of 1937 vintage, but the whole effect was spoilt by

the dull, unpolished radiator. The bus is on the 48 service from the Maypole and is in Longmore Street. 1060 is facing the Belgrave Road junction as it passes Mr Kinsman's newsagent, tobacconists and toy shop, which as well as selling tricycles, pedal cars and rocking horses has a large and very early large model of a London Transport Routemaster. Heresy! (A.B. Cross)

Just before the end of tramcar operation on the Moseley Road routes, totally enclosed Brush-bodied tram 726 has been painted in the final post-war version of the livery with small fleet numbers. The tram has just crossed Belgrave Road from Longmore Street and has just entered Gooch Street. The tram, working on the 37 service from Cannon Hill, will take the fairly sharp left turn in front of Pearks' grocery and provisions shop before

travelling along the remainder of Gooch Street's 600-yard long straight section and arriving at Sherlock Street. (F.N. Lloyd Jones)

One side of Gooch Street had already been demolished when 2066, (JOJ 66), sped towards Belgrave Road with its conductor carrying his Ultimate Ticket Machine and standing on the back platform. The bus is a Metro-Cammell-bodied Daimler CVD6 which is working on the 48J route which was the direct successor to the 39 tram route. Gooch Street had only recently been completed when the CBT began its steam tram operation on 19 July 1886 and until the redevelopment of the Highgate area in the 1960s, it was an area of small family concerns or local chains of shops such as A.D. Wimbush, George Mason's and Foster Brothers, the gentlemen's outfitters. (F.W. York)

The Triangle Cinema, on the corner of Gooch Street and Conybere Street was originally opened in 1913 as Pringles Picture Palace in premises which had previously been a chapel. It was the first cinema in Balsall Heath. The cinema was rebuilt in 1923 to the plans of Horace Bradley with 606 seats re-opening on 8 October 1923 with *The Pilgrim*, starring Charlie Chaplin. After its closure in 1959 it became the first Asian cinema in Birmingham. Woolworths had taken over a Victorian three-storey building next door to the cinema and put on to it their typical pre-war corporate name board and curved glass windows. Both premises were demolished during the wholesale redevelopment of the Balsall Heath area. (Birmingham Central Reference Library)

Unlike in neighbouring Edgbaston, land was sold off in Balsall Heath in a far more piecemeal fashion and when, in 1833, the landowner Revd Vincent Edwards died, it was a golden opportunity for Balsall Heath to develop rapidly. Car 728 turns from Gooch Street into Sherlock Street on the 39 service on 22 June 1949 when surrounded by derelict three-storey mid-Victorian premises which typified the sheer awfulness of the squeezing of as many properties as possible onto the smallest parcels of land. (Birmingham Central Reference Library)

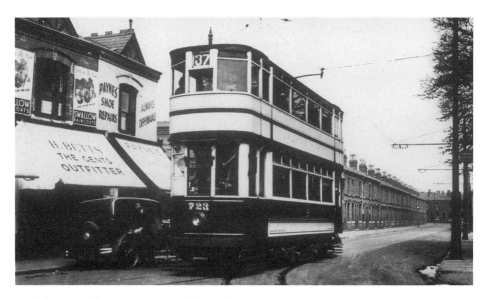

Both the 37 and the 39 tram routes followed the same route until they reached the Court Road–Edward Road junction. Brush totally enclosed EMB. Burnley bogie car 723, resplendent in its elaborate pre-war livery, but destined to have only a fourteen-year life being written-off after being badly damaged in the air raid on Witton depot on 4 December 1940, has reached the southern end of Court Road during April 1938. On the right are the trees which stood alongside the Cannon Hill public house while in the distance is the long terrace of 1870s housing reaching back to the distant Clevedon Road. (H.B. Priestley)

Another of the 40hp EMB Burnley bogie cars, car 731 has begun its little right and left shimmy across Edward Road and into the distant Cannon Hill Road, which was graced with superior, end-of-century, large Victorian villas. The 1926-built tram travels on an outbound 37 service. It has just passed Rawcliffe's newsagent and tobacconist's at the end of the short row of shops in Court Road. (A.J. Douglas, courtesy A.D. Packer)

Only two of the 401 class tramcars were repainted in grey livery. The first one to receive the grey was car 449, which was put into this livery in December 1942. The second tram was car 421, which was repainted once in April 1943 and again into fleet livery during August 1945. Despite the lack of blue paint, the paint shop at Kyotts Lake Road had given the grey a coat of varnish, so although the tram looked dowdy, it was still smart. Car 421 travels towards Cannon Hill Park in Cannon Hill Road when working on the 37 route. (Burrows Brothers)

Car 415 stands at the compulsory stop at the junction of Cannon Hill Road and Edgbaston Road in January 1943. The tram has all the wartime blackout restrictions while the street furniture is also suitably marked. The 37 tram route was little more than a large loop off the 'main line' 39 service through Balsall Heath and perhaps might have been a candidate for suspension during the Second World War but was retained; even so in wartime, the route ran only during peak periods. The 37 tram service completed its outward run by turning left into Edgbaston Park Road and after passing the entrance to Cannon Hill Park arrived at the terminus in Willows Road. (Burrows Brothers)

UEC-bodied radial truck car 130 has just come out of Cannon Hill Road and is standing in Edgbaston Road in about 1908. Behind the tram is the Warwickshire CC ground alongside the culvert of the River Rea. The Edgbaston ground was opened in 1886 and although it was briefly a Test Match venue during the Edwardian period, throughout the life of the 37 Cannon Hill tram route, no more Test Matches were played. From Court Road, the 37 route was a one-mile long, unidirectional, anticlockwise loop. Wingate H. Bett, the well-known ticket expert, termed such long loops on other systems as 'Cannon Hilling'. (Commercial postcard)

One of the prime reasons for the 37 tram route was to get passengers to and from Cannon Hill Park. The original 57.31 acres were donated to Birmingham by Miss Louisa Ryland and opened on 1 September 1873 and by the end of the century had been enlarged to over 80 acres. This lung of greenery was a

magnet for many years for people from all over Birmingham and in about 1930 was a beautifully mature and varied park. Today, Cannon Hill is Birmingham's premier park on the bank of the River Rea and still has the attraction of its Victorian greenhouses, its three lakes, a five-acre arboretum, a wild flower meadow and fine walks. Since 1960 it has been the venue for the famous spring Tulip Festival when up to 95,000 tulips are in flower. Since the 1960s the park has also been the home of the Midlands Art Centre. (Birmingham Central Reference Library)

The early 1920s affluent residences in Edgbaston Road opposite Cannon Hill Park overlooked the passage of the 37 trams for nearly thirty years until the route was abandoned on 1 October 1949. After that date only the 1A bus route travelled along this section of road as there was no equivalent replacement bus service. Car 730, a Brush-bodied EMB bogie car which had entered service in 1926, overtakes a 1937 Austin 10/4 Cambridge saloon as it travels towards the terminus of the 37 service in Willows Road. (G.F. Douglas)

Travelling over the tram tracks of the 37 Cannon Hill tram route in Edgbaston Park Road is bus 1261, (FOF 261). This 1939-vintage Daimler COG5 fitted with a Smethwick-built Birmingham Railway, Carriage and Wagon H30/24R body is working on the 1 short working route. The bus is opposite Cannon Hill Park and is almost at the Willows Road junction where the 37 tram terminus was located. 1261 will shortly begin the climb up Salisbury Road's steep hill before reaching its terminus in Moseley Village. (S.N.J. White)

On 29 May 1943, car 431 waits at the Willows Road terminus of the 37 route. This tram could easily be distinguished as it did not have opening top-ventilators. It had been used as a single-decker for the Nechells experiment with trailer cars and was fitted with a Kyotts Lake Road Works top cover in May 1923. Willows Road marked the edge of Balsall Heath and it represented the last of the 1880s-style two and three-storey terraced houses. Both the tram and the street furniture are marked out with blackout markings. (D.R. Harvey collection)

The terminus of the 37 route in Willows Road was an interesting urban boundary between the small Victorian terraced artisan housing and back-to-back courtyards found in much of Balsall Heath and the late Victorian large villas built for the white-collar workers in Moseley and King's Heath. Standing just inside Willows Road on 6 March 1948 is car 721 with the last of Balsall Heath's better-quality three-storey houses in the background. (R.B. Parr)

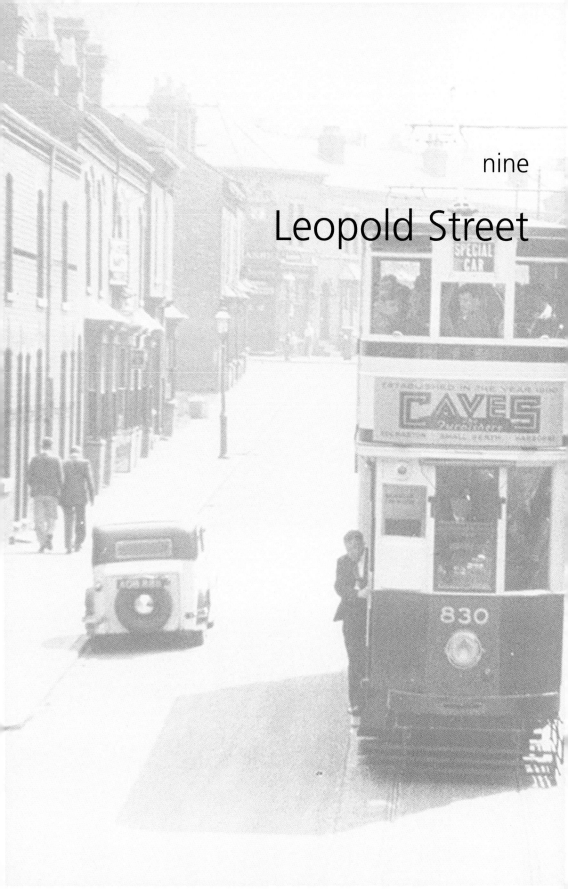

nine

Leopold Street

The 1920s White Swan public house stood next to a run down three-storey Victorian terrace on the southern corner of Hurst Street and Sherlock Street. On the opposite side are Edgar Shakeshaft's 'dining rooms' which are advertising hot sausage sandwiches. Car 401, the first of the class, travels into the short lower section of Hurst Street when working on the 41 service in 1948. On reaching the distant timber yard of Alfred Patterson's, the tram will turn right into Bishop Street before taking the left curve into MacDonald Street. (D.R. Harvey collection)

The driver of the 1949 Daimler CVD6 does his 'push and pull act' on the steering wheel as he hauls his charge out of Sherlock Street and into MacDonald Street. Bus 1962, (HOV 962), is being used on the 49B service, which was the shortest of the tram replacement bus services on the Moseley Road corridor. 1962 remained in service until the end of July 1964. Coming out of Wrentham Street is a Commer Superpoise 30cwt van owned by Hawleys Bread, a local company based at 192 Moseley Road. (R.F. Mack)

Coming out of Rea Street South after the 41 service tram has passed is a Birmingham-built Morris-Commercial 15cwt PV van – the PV meaning Parcels Van. Open-balcony car 419 is travelling along MacDonald Street out of the city away from Sherlock Street when working on the 41 service. Flanking the road are the grim three-storey terraces dating from the 1860s while beneath the brick parapets on both sides of MacDonald Street runs the culvert of the River Rea. On the left is the gateway to the former Anchor Bedstead factory. (J.H. Taylforth collection)

Opened in 1903, the impressive Rowton House was built in Alcester Street as a 'poor man's hotel', though it became little more than a hostel by the 1960s. It was later renamed the Highgate Hotel and in the 1980s it was transformed into the three-star, 250-room Chamberlain Park Hotel. Looking from Highgate Park at the side of Rowton House, in the summer of 1932, are the well-employed swings and the solitary roundabout, with some quite well-dressed local children enjoying themselves. Highgate Park was opened in 1876 by Joseph Chamberlain, the Mayor of Birmingham on a 4.37-acre site. The eastern end of the park opening on to Moseley Road had an extensive area of grass and tree-lined walks. (Birmingham Central Reference Library)

On 25 March 1952, bus 2058, (JOJ 58), has just crossed the junction with Vaughton Street as it travels over the long-abandoned tram tracks and the cobbled road surface in Thomas Street. This 'New-Look' front Daimler CVD6 travels into the city on the 49B service. These worn-out buildings were due to be replaced had the nearby pre-war St Martin's Flats pioneering complex not been prevented from being expanded by the outbreak of the Second World War. (Birmingham Public Works Department)

About to cross Vaughton Street from Thomas Street, with the Ansells-owned White House pub on the corner, is car 424, one of the fifty trams introduced in 1913 and modified for the 41 Leopold Street service's steep hill. In the foreground is the huge cleared site bounded by Vaughton Street, Emily Street and Dymoke Street. This clearance was completed by 1935 in preparation for the building of the St Martin's Flats housing complex which took three years to complete. The sheer squalor and drabness of the older Victorian houses, as well as the serious consequences of living in such unhealthy conditions, are awful to contemplate, yet much of the area through which car 424 had just travelled was to remain until the late 1960s. (D.R. Harvey collection)

St Martin's Flats were centred on Emily Street. Viewed from Leopold Street, this Eastern European-inspired development was completed in 1939 and consisted of 267 three and four-bedroom flats with balconies. They were a warning to future urban redevelopers and by the early 1960s the St Martin's complex was being termed as 'a run-down warren of problem flats'. They were demolished in 1981 and most of the replacement high-rise 1960s Highgate redevelopment areas properties have also been pulled down. (Birmingham Central Reference Library)

The tram's Spencer-Dawson air and oil brake, specifically fitted to the 401 class for use on the steep 1 in 13 Leopold Street, increased the tram's weight by 12cwt to 13 tons 2cwt and was designed to fail with the brakes locked on. The trams were fitted with Mountain and Gibson 7ft 6in. wheelbase trucks and being low-height cars at 15ft 7½in. high, could be used anywhere on the system. Car 436 picks up passengers at the junction with Dymoke Street. The stark, factory-like building is St Alban's National School while on the other side of Leopold Street is Mrs Annie Hardy's newsagent shop on the corner of Dymoke Street. (F.N. Lloyd Jones)

Car 422 takes the curve just above Samuel Heath's brass works when descending the 1 in 13 hill in Leopold Street during 1948. In the distance, contrasting with the old Victorian properties, are the St Martin's Flats of 1939, which in later years caused serious structural and social problems which were to be repeated in the high-rise properties built in the 1960s. The lorry coming out of Heath's factory is of wartime American origin and is probably a GMC or a Dodge. (F.N. Lloyd Jones)

The steepest part of Leopold Street was largely devoted to heavy industry, with Samuel Heath's brass works on the left and Pressman's Cupro Foundry which manufactured aluminium ingot alloys at the top of the hill. Car 427 begins its descent of Leopold Street when working on the 41 service into the city in 1948. (D.R. Harvey collection)

On 1 October 1949, which was the last day of operation, enclosed car 729 has notices of the Moseley Road tramway abandonment pasted in the balcony windows as it is driven up the steepest 1 in 13 section of Leopold Street. The brass foundry factory of Samuel Heath was set up in Leopold Street in 1830 and still remains there in the twenty-first century. Heaths were most famous for the brass clock which was their centre piece at the Great Exhibition of 1851. (F.N. Lloyd Jones)

Turning out of Leopold Street into Moseley Road is outbound car 408. It is working on the 40 service to High Street, King's Heath. Almost hidden by the trees is the decorative brickwork of the Society of Friends' Hall and Institute which was constructed at the expense of Richard Cadbury in 1899. In front of the tram is bus 1660, (HOV 660), an almost new Leyland Titan PD2/1 with a Brush body which is working on the express 35 bus service to the Maypole. (D.R. Harvey Collection)

Other local titles published by Tempus

The Inner Circle: Birmingham's No. 8 Bus Route

MAGGIE HANSON, DAVID HARVEY AND PETER DRAKE

This superb collection of over 200 old photographs illustrates the changes seen along the Inner Circle bus route over the years. It also shows the buses that have worked on it so it is guaranteed to fascinate bus enthusiasts but will also have huge appeal for the thousands of Brummies who have ever travelled the route. This is an unusual book that will have wide appeal for anyone interested in Birmingham's history.

0 7524 2636 2

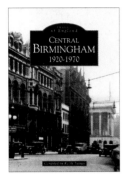

Central Birmingham 1920-1970

KEITH TURNER

This collection of over 200 photographs of central Birmingham will fascinate all those who have ever lived or worked in the city. Much has changed over this period of time and this splendid sequence of images catalogues many of them beautifully.

0 7524 0340 0

Central Birmingham Pubs: Volumes 1 & 2

JOESEPH MCKENNA

These two volumes on the history of the inns and public houses of Birmingham's central area provide a comprehensive background to the history of drinking establishments in the city. Lost pubs, converted pubs, changes of use and their social history are all included. The books are well indexed and provide a valuable reference source for drinkers and historians!

0 7524 3873 5 / 0 7524 4144 2

Haunted Birmingham

ARTHUR SMITH AND RACHEL BANNISTER

From creepy happenings in the city centre to stories of phantoms in the theatres, pubs and hospitals, this book contains a chilling range of ghostly tales. Drawing on historical and contemporary sources the authors tell of a landlady who haunts her old pub, two dead workmen who came back to haunt the Town Hall and an ex-mayor who still watches over the city. Scary stuff!

0 7524 4017 9

If you are interested in purchasing other books published by Tempus, or in case you have difficulty finding any Tempus books in your local bookshop, you can also place orders directly through our website

www.tempus-publishing.com